D1527171

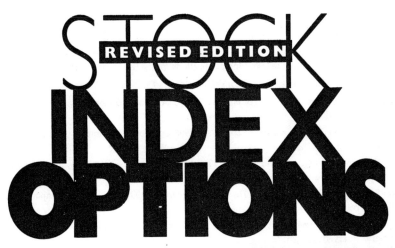

STOCK
REVISED EDITION
INDEX
OPTIONS

HOW TO
USE AND
PROFIT FROM
INDEXED
OPTIONS IN
VOLATILE &
UNCERTAIN
MARKETS

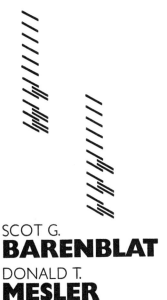

SCOT G.
BARENBLAT
DONALD T.
MESLER

PROBUS PUBLISHING COMPANY
Chicago, Illinois
Cambridge, England

The authors wish to thank the following publications for the use of materials.

Page 43: *The New York Times,* August 25, 1991. © 1990 by *The New York Times.*

Page 69: Reprinted by permission of *Barron's* © 1990 Dow Jones & Company, Inc. All rights reserved worldwide.

Page 73: Reprinted by permission of *Barron's* © 1990 Dow Jones & Company, Inc. All rights reserved worldwide.

Page 76: Reprinted by permission of *Barron's* © 1990 Dow Jones & Company, Inc. All rights reserved worldwide.

Page 86: Reprinted by permission of *The Wall Street Journal* © 1991 Dow Jones & Company, Inc. All rights reserved worldwide.

Page 89: Reprinted by permission of *The Wall Street Journal* © 1991 Dow Jones & Company, Inc. All rights reserved worldwide.

ISBN 1-55862-181-x

Printed in the United States of America

KP

1 2 3 4 5 6 7 8 9 0

SGB's corner
To Elise & Benjamin

DTM's corner
To My Mother & Father

Contents

APPENDIXES:

PREFACE

Nearly everyone, from taxicab drivers to corporate executives, has an opinion about the direction of the stock market. However, relatively few people have clear or sophisticated ideas about the translation of these opinions into well conceived market positions. This book focuses on stock index options as a powerful vehicle for effecting this translation. Index options enable stock market participants to place market bets and/or hedge current holdings quickly, conveniently, and efficiently.

The growth and popularity of these instruments is a testament to their usefulness. Stock index options didn't exist in this country in January of 1983. Today, index options trade on seventeen different market indexes at five different market exchanges. Trading volume for the most popular index option, the Standard & Poors 100 Index option, today exceeds the trading volume on the New York Stock Exchange in terms of underlying assets controlled. Stock index options are one of the most successful financial products of the decade.

This book explores index options in depth sufficient to enable investors to confidently direct transactions and brokers and advisors to recommend positions responsibly. The intention of the book is to provide a working knowledge which can be applied immediately in the marketplace. The reader will learn:

How do stock index options work?
How do the underlying stock indexes differ?
How do stock index options differ from listed stock options?
How should investors analyze stock index option strategies?

How can stock index options:
    protect against declining markets?
    capitalize on both bull and bear markets?
    capitalize on market volatility?
How are stock index options priced?
How can investors synthetically create stock index options?

This book is organized assuming the reader has no prior knowledge of options theory. Chapter 1 provides an overview of the marketplace and discusses the role of stock index options for hedgers and speculators. Chapters 2 and 3 discuss construction and composition of important stock indexes in detail. These chapters highlight differences between underlying indexes to help investors select the best index option. Chapter 4 covers options mechanics. It makes clear the distinctions between stock index options and listed stock options, and establishes a conceptual framework for thinking about options in terms of payoff profiles.

In Chapter 5 the concepts developed earlier are combined to explore classic option strategies. Using actual options quotations from financial publications and real world events to guide investment outlook, the reader will discover how stock and/or options positions are combined to produce well conceived market positions. Eleven separate strategies are discussed, and seven are worked through in careful detail. The detailed examples illustrate clearly the type of analysis which is appropriate to investors contemplating the use of index options. Chapter 6 extends the discussion to a class of newly introduced long term stock index options.

Chapter 7 explores index option valuation with a simple but complete review of the Black-Scholes formula. Chapter 8 expands the discussion to produce a mechanism for synthetic index option replication. Chapter 9 provides a brief review of topics for special consideration.

The Appendixes at the end of the book are a detailed compilation of available historical and current information on index options. These charts, tables, and contract specifications are a valuable resource for quick reference. A thorough bibliography on indexes and options is provided for those wishing to pursue these subjects in further detail.

We wish to express thanks to Monitor Capital Advisors and New York Life Insurance Company for providing the supportive and constructive professional environment which spawned this project and nourished it through months of construction and revision. We are also grateful to Ronald J. Sunog for his productive critique of the preliminary manuscript.

Scot G. Barenblat
Donald T. Mesler
New York

1

Overview

In January of 1982, it was difficult to translate a market opinion quickly into a well conceived wager on the market. Investors who sought to assume market exposures consistent with near or long term investment outlook had available to them alternatives such as concentrated portfolios of stock, diversified portfolios of stock, stock mutual funds, and options on individual stocks. Unfortunately, none of those alternatives were completely satisfying. Most importantly, none were certain to achieve performance which coincided precisely with any well defined market. In addition, they were unnecessarily either risky, time consuming, or inflexible.

Today however, several products are available which permit strategists to take positions quickly on well specified markets. In addition, these products provide investors the advantages of high leverage, low transaction costs, and deep liquidity. These products include stock index futures, options on stock index futures, and stock index options.

These instruments have many analogous characteristics, making them similarly well suited for a variety of investment strategies. Despite their similarities, each remains sufficiently unique and complex that students and investors normally approach them individually. Further, these instruments are not equally accessible. Stock index options are the most accessible of the three because they can be traded through a stockbroker in a regular margin account. Stock index futures and options on stock index futures must be traded through a commodities broker in a commodities account. For these reasons, this book will address stock index options exclusively.

OPTIONABLE INDEXES

Currently, stock index options are traded on 17 different indexes, where an index is defined as a composite of stocks. These indexes are listed in Exhibit 1-1. While mastery of options theory is the most obvious challenge facing investors contemplating the use of index options, selection of the appropriate underlying index is also formidable. The seventeen optionable indexes have vastly different characteristics, causing them to respond differently to changing domestic

EXHIBIT 1-1

Optionable Indexes

American Stock Exchange Computer Technology
American Stock Exchange Institutional
American Stock Exchange International Market
American Stock Exchange Japan
American Stock Exchange Major Market
American Stock Exchange LT-20
American Stock Exchange Oil
Financial News Composite
New York Stock Exchange Composite
Philadelphia Stock Exchange Gold & Silver
Philadelphia Stock Exchange National Over-the-Counter
Philadelphia Stock Exchange Utility
Standard & Poor's 100
Chicago Board Options Exchange OEX-LEAPS
Standard & Poor's 500
Chicago Board Options Exchange SPX-LEAPS
Value Line Composite

and world events. For speculators it is critical to select the index which participates in an expected market move. For hedgers it is critical to select the index which mirrors movement of the portfolio being protected. A thorough review of optionable indexes is presented in Chapters 2 & 3, and this review describes criteria upon which the selection decision should be based.

PREVIEW OF STRATEGIES

A familiarity with listed stock options makes an understanding of index options relatively simple. However, such a familiarity is not assumed in this text and options mechanics are presented in detail. In general, buying and selling index options is like buying and selling listed stock options. For this reason, index options can be used to implement most of the strategies typically employed using listed options. However, unlike listed options, index options require cash settlement. This unique feature of index options trading introduces unique risks not found in listed options trading. Fortunately, these risks are easily understandable and manageable. They are discussed in detail in Chapter 4.

Given a grasp of the vehicle and an understanding of the risks, the investor is ready to survey potential applications for stock index options. A representative sample includes the following:

1 Speculate on the overall market.
2 Speculate on segments of the market.
3 Hedge an equity portfolio in anticipation of market decline.
4 Position a portfolio for large market moves while generating additional investment income.
5 Separate market risk from stock and industry group risk.
6 Establish a market position prior to receipt of funds.

These applications are implemented using classic options techniques which are well established in the market. However, the presentation of these strategies in Chapter 5 develops a method of analysis which will enable creative investors to devise their own strategies as well. Two additional strategies tailored to the use of newly introduced long term index options are presented in Chapter 6.

Some of the most exciting prospects for index options are applications in conjunction with indexed mutual funds. These funds are only recently available to retail investors. Indexed mutual funds are registered investment companies specifically designed to track a particular index benchmark. Among optionable indexes, only mutual funds linked to the Standard & Poor's 500 Index are presently available. However, mutual funds linked to other optionable indexes are likely to be introduced in the future. Indexed mutual funds provide an excellent vehicle for creation of synthetic index options. Synthetic option strategies might be used when real options are unavailable or too expensive. Chapter 8 discusses one such strategy.

LOOKING AHEAD

Indexing technology has developed at a rapid pace during the past decade, reflecting an increasing awareness of indexes by participants in the financial markets. This improving technology has made indexes ever better representatives of designated markets. Index options enable investors to latch on to this growing technology base because they offer market exposures which are precisely tied to the behavior of these carefully constructed market measures. For hedgers, index options offer an efficient and cost effective mechanism for protecting portfolios from the volatility of the markets. For speculators, index options offer a similarly effective means for assuming well conceived market positions likely to achieve performance which coincides favorably with an identified target market. The information needed by both groups to effectively use these vehicles in the marketplace is presented in the chapters which follow.

2

Index Construction

The role of indexes in the capital markets has grown steadily over the past decade. Long used by professional money managers as benchmarks for general market performance, indexes today are highly specialized measurement tools which enhance and support the business of brokerage firms, investment banks, and financial publishers. As their usage has expanded, investors at all levels have become increasingly aware of their importance. Notably, the recent introduction of passively managed indexed mutual funds for retail investors evidences the growth of this awareness among the broad investing public. However, while investor awareness of indexes has improved, investor understanding of them has not. Many investors remain confused about what indexes represent and how they are constructed.

This chapter provides an investor tutorial on indexes, emphasizing those indexes which underlie stock index options. The importance of this material is evident if one recognizes that investors in stock index options are actually making bets on the future price movement of the indexes underneath the options. These indexes are differentiable in terms of their design and purpose, making each appropriate to certain situations and inappropriate to others. This chapter outlines these differences and highlights practical implications. A working knowledge of the theory of indexes will not only improve investor understanding of an increasingly valuable capital market tool, but will assist investors in selecting a stock index option tailored to exploit a particular market outlook.

INDEX DESIGN

Several designs for indexes have been developed. Hence there is diversity in the calculation, weighting, and number and type of stocks included. A brief review of key design alternatives follows.

Averages Versus Indexes

There are two predominant methods used for calculation of stock market indicators: averaging and indexing. An average is simply the mean value of a group of stock prices. An index on the other hand is an average expressed in terms of a base value (usually 100) established at some previous point in time. Although related, these two forms are distinct and impart slightly different attributes to market indicators.

Despite their differences, investors generally cannot differentiate between averages and indexes, thus confusion and misperception often surround their use. Among presently optionable indexes, only the American Stock Exchange Major Market Index is a true average while the rest are true indexes. Throughout this book the term index is used when discussing market indicators generally or true market indexes specifically. The term average is used only when discussing indicators which are true averages.

Price Weighting Versus Cap Weighting

There are two predominant weighting schemes given to stock market indicators: price weighting or capitalization weighting. Either weighting scheme can be applied to averages or indexes. Price weighting is preferred for measuring changes in stock prices and therefore is commonly used as an indicator of performance for a group of stocks. The value of a price weighted average is calculated by (i) determining the sum of all stock prices, and (ii) dividing by the "average divisor." The average value is converted to an index value by (i) dividing by the

6

EXHIBIT 2-1

Price Weighted Indicator Calculation - Base Period

Stock	Price
A	20
B	40
C	60
Sum	120

Average Divisor =	3
Average Value = (Sum/Average Divsor) = (120/3) =	40
Index Divisor = Base Period Average =	40
Factor =	100
Index Value = (Average Value/Index Divisor)*(Factor) = (40/40)*(100) =	100

EXHIBIT 2-2

Price Weighted Indicator Calculation - Subsequent Period

Stock	Price
A	40
B	80
C	120
Sum	240

Average Divisor =	3
Average Value = (Sum/Average Divsor) = (240/3) =	80
Index Divisor = Base Period Average =	40
Factor =	100
Index Value = (Average Value/Index Divisor)*(Factor) = (80/40)*(100) =	200

"index divisor" (which is the average value at the base period) and (ii) multiplying by a factor selected to be the index base value, traditionally 100. Exhibit 2-1 illustrates the computation of a price weighted

EXHIBIT 2-3

Price Weighted Indicator Distortions - 2:1 Split of Stock C

Stock	Price
A	40
B	80
C	60
Sum	180

Average Divisor =	3
Average Value = (Sum/Average Divsor) = (180/3) =	60
Index Divisor = Base Period Average =	40
Factor =	100
Index Value = (Average Value/Index Divisor)*(Factor) = (60/40)*(100) =	150

average and index in the base period. Exhibit 2-2 illustrates the procedure for a subsequent period assuming all stock prices have doubled.

Although the computations for maintaining a price weighted indicator are normally straightforward, complications arise when a component stock price is adjusted by the exchange where it is listed due to events which are unrelated to the market forces of supply and demand. The most common of these events are stock splits or stock dividends. Unless a corresponding computational adjustment is made, distortions in the indicator will appear which are not representative of the actual fortunes of the companies involved. Exhibit 2-3 demonstrates the distortion which occurs if no computational adjustments are made for a 2 for 1 split of stock C. Notice that both indicator values dropped significantly but there was no fundamental change in the value of issue C to shareholders. Thus the indicators calculated are erroneous.

The most common way to compensate for price adjusting events is to alter the divisor such that the indicator value after the event equals the indicator value before the event. Continuing from the previous exhibit, Exhibit 2-4 illustrates the required adjustment for price

EXHIBIT 2-4

Price Weighted Indicator Calculation - 2:1 Split of Stock C

Stock	Price
A	40
B	80
C	60
Sum	180

Adjusted Average Divisor =	2.25
Adjusted Average Value = (Sum/Adjusted Average Divsor) = (180/2.25) =	80
Adjusted Index Divisor =	30
Factor =	100
Adjusted Index Value = (Average Value/Index Divisor)*(Factor) = (60/30)*(100) =	200

weighted indicators given the hypothetical 2 for 1 split of stock C. The exhibit shows that by adjusting the average divisor to 2.25, the average value after the split equals the average value prior to the split. The exhibit also shows that by adjusting the index divisor to 30, the index value after the split equals the index value prior to the split. Similarly, the divisor is adjusted to maintain continuity when stock dividends are paid. A third non-market event which triggers divisor adjustment is a change in the stocks comprising the indicator.

The second predominant weighting scheme given to stock market indicators is capitalization weighting. Cap weighting is preferred for measuring changes in the value of companies and therefore is commonly used as an indicator of prosperity for the overall economy. Cap weighted indicators combine and reflect changes in the capitalizations of all the companies in the indicator, where capitalization is defined as the total market value of all outstanding stock. A cap weighted indicator is calculated exactly like a price weighted indicator except that capitalizations are used instead of stock prices. Exhibit 2-5 illustrates the base period procedure.

Like price weighted indicators, the divisor for a cap weighted

EXHIBIT 2-5

Capitalization Weighted Indicator Calculation - Base Period

Stock	Price	Shares Outstanding	Capitalization
A	20	500,000	10,000,000
B	40	2,000,000	80,000,000
C	60	3,000,000	180,000,000
Sum			270,000,000

Average Divisor =	3
Average Value = (Sum/Average Divisor) = (270,000,000/3) =	90,000,000

Index Divisor = Base Period Average =	90,000,000
Factor =	100
Index Value = (Average Value/Index Divisor)*(Factor) =	
(90,000,000/90,000,000)*(100) =	100

EXHIBIT 2-6

Capitalization Weighted Indicator Calculation - Issuance of One Million Shares of Stock C

Stock	Price	Shares Outstanding	Capitalization
A	20	500,000	10,000,000
B	40	2,000,000	80,000,000
C	60	4,000,000	240,000,000
Sum			330,000,000

Adjusted Average Divisor =	3.67
Adjusted Average Value = (Sum/Adjusted Average Divisor) =	
(330,000,000/3.67) =	90,000,000

Adjusted Index Divisor =	110,000,000
Factor =	100
Adjusted Index Value = (Average Value/AdjustedIndex Divisor)*(Factor) =	
(110,000,000/110,000,000)*(100) =	100

index or average is subject to frequent change. However, *while the divisor of a price weighted indicator is changed when the price of a component stock is artificially adjusted, the divisor of a cap weighted indicator is changed when the capitalization of a component stock is artificially adjusted.* The most common capitalization changing event is the issue of additional stock. To compensate for the additional stock, the divisor is adjusted such that the indicator value after the issuance is equal to the indicator value before the issuance. Continuing from the previous exhibit, Exhibit 2-6 illustrates the adjustment procedure required for cap weighted indicators given a hypothetical issuance of one million shares of stock C.

Notice that the issuance of additional stock increases the market capitalization of stock C by $60,000,000. The exhibit shows that by adjusting the average divisor to 3.67, the average value after the split equals the average value prior to the split. The exhibit also shows that by adjusting the index divisor to 110,000,000, the index value after the split equals the index value prior to the split. This procedure makes intuitive sense because the increase in capitalization of C associated with the stock issuance does not reflect any change in fundamental value to shareholders.

INDEX PURPOSE

Indexes are intended as market indicators. They are supposed to gauge the overall level of stock prices usually by measuring performance of a representative sample of individual stocks. While simple enough in concept, this objective is difficult to implement. The final conclusions from any foray into index study are that no index is perfect in every respect, no index is suitable for all applications, and no index will replicate its behavior relative to other indexes on every occasion.

Broad-Based Indexes

The indexes that underlie index options can be classified into two major groups: broad-based and narrow-based. Broad-based indexes are those that are composed of a large number of stocks with the

EXHIBIT 2-7

Broad-Based Optionable Indexes

American Stock Exchange Institutional
American Stock Exchange International Market
American Stock Exchange Japan
American Stock Exchange Major Market
American Stock Exchange LT-20
Financial News Composite
New York Stock Exchange Composite
Philadelphia Stock Exchange National Over-the-Counter
Standard & Poor's 100
Chicago Board Options Exchange OEX-LEAPS
Standard & Poor's 500
Chicago Board Options Exchange SPX-LEAPS
Value Line Composite

objective of reflecting movements in large or generalized markets. Among the optionable indexes, thirteen are broad-based and are listed in Exhibit 2-7. In most cases, the exchanges themselves have developed these indexes as platforms for derivative products (such as index options) with the intention of creating needed investment products and generating additional trading activity. Indexes in this category are readily identifiable because their names include the name of the exchange/developer. Exceptions are the Financial News Composite introduced by the Financial News Network on which options are traded at the Pacific Stock Exchange, the Value Line Composite developed by the Value Line Investment Survey on which options are traded at the Philadelphia Stock Exchange, and the indexes maintained by Standard & Poors Company on which options are traded at the Chicago Board Options Exchange. A brief description of each broad-based index follows and a complete description of each is given in Appendix A.

American Stock Exchange Institutional Index

A capitalization weighted index of the 75 stocks currently held in the greatest dollar amounts among institutional equity portfolios. This index is designed to track the performance of core stock holdings of large scale institutional investors.

American Stock Exchange International Market Index

A capitalization weighted index of 50 leading foreign stocks from 10 countries and 20 industry groups. This index is designed to measure the performance of the broad international economy.

American Stock Exchange Japan Index

A modified price weighted index of 210 common stocks actively traded on the Tokyo Stock Exchange. This index is designed to measure economic performance of the overall Japanese economy.

American Stock Exchange Major Market Index

A price weighted arithmetic average of 20 major blue chip stocks representative of major US industrial corporations. This index is designed to mirror the movements of the Dow Jones Industrial Average, which is also calculated as a price weighted average.

American Stock Exchange LT-20 Index:

A price weighted arithmetic average of 20 major blue chip stocks representative of major US industrial corporations. Calculated as 1/20th of the Major Market Index, this index is designed to mirror precisely the movements of the Major Market but at a lower index price level.

Financial News Composite Index

A price weighted index of 30 large capitalization stocks listed on the New York Stock Exchange. This index is also designed to mirror the movements of the Dow Jones Industrial Average.

New York Stock Exchange Composite Index

A capitalization weighted index of all 1600+ common stocks listed on the New York Stock Exchange. This index is designed to measure changes in the aggregate market value of NYSE common stocks.

Philadelphia Stock Exchange National Over-the-Counter Index
A capitalization weighted index of the 100 largest over the counter stocks. This index is designed to mirror the movements of the NASDAQ-OTC Composite Index.

Standard & Poor's 100 Index
A capitalization weighted index of 100 stocks from a broad range of industries. This index is designed to measure changes in the market value of the largest 100 stocks for which options are currently listed on the CBOE.

Chicago Board Options Exchange OEX-LEAPS Index
A capitalization weighted index of 100 stocks from a broad range of industries. Calculated as 1/10th of the S&P 100 Index, this index is designed to mirror precisely the movements of the S&P 100 but at a lower index price level.

Standard & Poor's 500 Index
A capitalization weighted index of 500 stocks from a broad range of industries. This index is designed to measure changes in the market value of 500 stocks representing all major industries in approximately the same proportion to their representation on the New York Stock Exchange.

Chicago Board Options Exchange SPX-LEAPS Index
A capitalization weighted index of 500 stocks from a broad range of industries. Calculated as 1/10th of the S&P 500 Index, this index is designed to mirror precisely the movements of the S&P 500 but at a lower index price level.

Value Line Composite Index
A price weighted index of all 1700+ stocks followed by the Value Line Investment Survey. This index is designed to measure changes in the universe of primarily second tier stocks followed by the Survey.

Narrow-based Indexes

The second major group of indexes that underlie index options are those that are narrow based. Narrow-based indexes, also called subindexes, are typically composed of smaller numbers of stocks and have the objective of reflecting movements in small or focused markets. Among the optionable indexes, four are narrow-based and are listed in Exhibit 2-8. As is clear from their names, all of these indexes were developed by the exchanges on which their options trade. A brief description of each narrow-based index follows and a complete description of each is given in Appendix A.

American Stock Exchange Computer Technology Index

A capitalization weighted index of 30 widely held stocks representing various segments of the computer industry. This index is designed to measure the performance of the computer industry on whole.

American Stock Exchange Oil Index

A price weighted index of 16 widely held stocks representing various segments of the oil industry. This index is designed to measure the performance of the oil industry on whole.

Philadelphia Stock Exchange Gold & Silver Index

A capitalization weighted index of 7 companies involved in gold and silver mining and production. This index is designed to measure the performance of the gold and silver mining industry on whole.

EXHIBIT 2-8

Narrow-Based Optionable Indexes

American Stock Exchange Computer Technology
American Stock Exchange Oil
Philadelphia Stock Exchange Gold & Silver
Philadelphia Stock Exchange Utility

Philadelphia Stock Exchange Utility Index

A capitalization weighted index of 20 geographically diverse utility companies. This index is designed to measure the performance of the utility industry on whole.

PRACTICAL IMPLICATIONS

The foregoing review of index theory establishes a context for discussion of the indicators underlying stock index options. The different purpose and design features which distinguish indicators cause them to respond differently to changing market conditions. Given this understanding of basic index theory, consider the following practical implications.

Concentration

It should be clear by now that stocks with the highest prices have the greatest influence in a price weighted indicator while stocks with the largest market capitalizations have the greatest influence in a cap weighted indicator. However, it is not immediately apparent that dominance of an indicator by a small group of component stocks is generally problematic only with cap weighting. This is because market capitalizations typically vary more substantially between stocks than do market prices. The following example illustrates this idea.

Recall that the Philadelphia Stock Exchange Utility Index is a capitalization weighted index of 20 geographically diverse utility companies designed to measure the performance of the overall utility industry. In April of 1990 the three largest cap companies — Pacific Gas & Electric, Southern California Edison, and The Southern Company — comprised over 25% of the total capitalization of the index even though they represented only 15% of the stocks. This is because their capitalizations were substantially greater than those of the other component stocks. However, if this index had been price weighted they would have comprised only 16% of the index because their prices were not significantly different from those of other component stocks. One would expect the cap weighted Utility Index to be dominated by the performance of these three largest companies.

The precise influence of a component stock upon a cap weighted index can be calculated by computing the number of "shares of the stock in the index." This is achieved by dividing the total shares outstanding for that stock by the index divisor. Continuing the previous example, the total shares outstanding for Pacific Gas & Electric was 426,667,000 and the Utility Index divisor was 465,413,145 making the shares of PG&E in the index equal to 0.92. Thus, if PG&E had increased by one point, the value of the index would have increased by 0.92.

Investors in index options should understand that cap weighted indexes can and will be dominated by the largest cap stocks. Investors should explore these stocks prior to investment in index options, and should monitor these stocks over the life of the option. A listing of stocks contained in an index along with corresponding outstanding shares, cap weights and the most recent divisor can be obtained by writing the exchanges on which options for the index are traded (Appendix D).

Price Levels

A second implication of the foregoing is that indexes will have different price levels. Price levels depend primarily upon the initial base value chosen for the index. Although 100 is traditionally chosen as the base, no particular price level is considered optimal. However, price levels do make a difference because lower priced indexes result in smaller option contract values. Therefore, more contracts on a lower priced index must be purchased to obtain dollar exposure equal to that obtained with fewer contracts on a higher priced index. Because they correspond to relatively small dollar exposures, options on lower priced indexes are generally well suited to investors seeking to hedge or speculate on smaller positions. The price level of an underlying index is an important consideration which can justifiably influence the index selection decision.

IMPORTANT NON-OPTIONABLE INDEXES

Thus far the discussion has been restricted to the seventeen optionable indexes. However, these represent only a small portion of the total number of indexes that have been developed. Brokerage firms, investment advisers, and financial publishers maintain numerous other indexes that have varying degrees of usefulness and popularity. Three of these non-optionable indexes are particularly important because they are widely followed and/or measure a different aspect of the overall market. They are the Dow Jones Industrial Aver-

EXHIBIT 2-9

Features of Optionable & Non-Optionable Indexes

Index	Issues	Design
American Stock Exchange Computer Technology	30	Narrow
American Stock Exchange Institutional	75	Broad
American Stock Exchange International Market	50	Broad
American Stock Exchange Japan	210	Broad
American Stock Exchange Major Market	20	Broad
American Stock Exchange Oil	16	Narrow
Financial News Composite	30	Broad
New York Stock Exchange Composite	1600+	Broad
Philadelphia Stock Exchange Gold & Silver	7	Narrow
Philadelphia Stock Exchange National Over-the-Counter	100	Broad
Philadelphia Stock Exchange Utility	20	Narrow
Standard & Poors 100	100	Broad
Standard & Poors 500	500	Broad
Value Line Composite	1700+	Broad
Dow Jones Industrial	30	Broad
NASDAQ-OTC Composite	3600+	Broad
Wilshire 5000 Equity	5000+	Broad

* Three separate S&P 500 contracts are available: the SPX, SPL, and NSX.

SPX & SPL values are based on closing index levels, while NSX values are based on opening index levels.

SPX maturities are available for six months: two nearby and up to four from the March quarterly cycle.

NSX maturities are available for three months from the March quarterly cycle only.

age, the NASDAQ-OTC, and the Wilshire 5000 Equity Index. Although options are not available for these indexes, they may be useful in other ways and it is interesting to put them in perspective with the optionable indexes. A brief description of each non-optionable index follows and a complete description of each is given in Appendix B.

Dow Jones Industrial Average

A price weighted arithmetic average of 30 high quality stocks compiled by Dow Jones & Company and published by the *Wall Street Journal* and its sister publication *Barron's National Business & Financial*

Type	Weight	Base Date	BaseValue	Option Symbol	Options Exchange
Index	Cap	7/29/83	100	XCI	Amex
Index	Cap	6/24/86	250	XII	Amex
Index	Cap	1/2/87	200	ADR	Amex
Index	Price	4/2/90	280	JPN	Amex
Average	Price	#	#	XMI	Amex
Index	Price	8/27/84	125	XOI	Amex
Index	Price	+	+	FNC	PSE
Index	Cap	12/31/65	50	NYA	NYSE
Index	Cap	12/19/83	100	XAU	PHLX
Index	Cap	9/28/84	150	XOC	PHLX
Index	Cap	+	+	UTY	PHLX
Index	Cap	1/2/76	100	OEX	CBOE
Index	Cap	1941-3	10	*SPX	CBOE
Index	Price	6/30/61	100	VLE	PHLX
Average	Cap	#	#		
Index	Cap	2/5/71	100		
Index	Cap	12/31/80	1404.6		

SPL maturities are available for two months (June & December) at 25 point intervals for up to two years.

SPX is the most liquid, and is the option intended for discussion in this book.

\# Only indexes have base dates and base values; these measures are inappropriate to averages.

\+ Unavailable at time of writing.

Weekly. This index is designed to track the performance of dominant domestic industrial corporations.

NASDAQ-OTC Composite Index

A capitalization weighted index of all 3600+ over-the-counter stocks listed on the the National Association of Securities Dealers Automated Quotation system. This index is designed to measure changes in the aggregate market value of NASDAQ common stocks.

Wilshire 5000 Equity Index

A capitalization weighted index of all 5000+ actively traded common stocks in the United States. This index is designed to reflect the performance of the stock market in the broadest sense.

LOOKING AHEAD

This concludes the basic examination of index construction. Exhibit 2-9 summarizes much of the information discussed thus far. In Chapter 3 the analysis is extended by focusing on the historical price movements of broad-based indexes.

3

Index Price Movement

Chapter 2 outlined the ways in which available indexes differ. Various indexes were shown to measure different markets or limited segments of particular markets. Further, different index calculation and weighting methods were demonstrated. The analysis led to the conclusions that indexes do not move in lock step, and discrimination is required when choosing an index to insure that its behavior is best suited to the purpose of the investor.

The narrow-based index selection decision is clear cut because subindexes are tailored to reflect the movements of well defined domestic market segments: computer technology, petroleum products, gold and silver, and utilities. However, the broad-based index selection decision is more difficult because all broad-based indexes are intended to reflect the movement of the overall market.

Given their considerable differences, investors might reasonably ask which broad market index is best suited to a particular investment objective. This chapter addresses this question by comparing the historical price movements of the broad-based indexes. An examination of the ways in which their differences have impacted price movements will provide insight into the character of the broad-based indexes and will assist investors in the broad-based index selection decision.

CHART ANALYSIS

Charting is one of the best ways to gain insight into the comovement between indexes because it is immediately and intuitively revealing. Exhibits 3-1 through 3-10 display the results of a careful charting analysis process applied to the domestic broad-based indexes identified in Chapter 2. Before proceeding to these pages, the reader should be aware of the following methodological decisions underlying the analysis.

Methodology

For purposes of the analysis, each broad-based indicator was re-indexed to a base value of 100 at the beginning of the historical period under consideration. This technique has the advantage of making movements between indexes with different absolute levels directly comparable. However, this approach has the disadvantage that the actual quoted index value is lost thus creating potential for confusion in interpretation. Readers should understand that the index levels shown on the charts are relative and not absolute.

Whenever possible, a ten year historical horizon ending December 31, 1990 was used. The ten year history was chosen to be as recent as possible given the time lag to publication and because it encompasses a wide range of market conditions and circumstances. The time horizon includes the very weak stock prices prevalent in mid-1982, the great bull market of the 1980's which started in August of 1982, the stock market crash of October 1987, the mini-crash of October 1989, and market response to the Iraqi invasion of Kuwait in August of 1990. Shorter records were used in situations for which ten years of data were unavailable.

Finally, the Standard & Poors 500 Stock Index was chosen as a benchmark for comparison. The selection of a benchmark eliminates the need to overlay each index with every other index, making the presentation more manageable. The S&P 500 was chosen because it is most widely used in the investment industry as a performance standard.

Broad-Based Juxtaposition

Exhibit 3-1 shows the AMEX Institutional versus the S&P 500. Recall that the Institutional is comprised of those stocks held in the greatest dollar amount by institutional equity investors. Therefore, the extremely close comovement between these two indexes may reflect the tendency among institutional money managers to hold those stocks which dominate the S&P.

Exhibit 3-2 shows the AMEX Major Market versus the S&P 500. Recall that the Major Market is designed to replicate the behavior of the Dow Jones Industrial Average. The comovement between these two indexes is close; however, the chart reveals that the smaller stocks of the S&P 500 underperformed the larger stocks of the Major Market during the entire period.

Exhibit 3-3 shows the Financial News Composite versus the S&P 500. Recall that the FNC is also designed to replicate the behavior of the Dow. The extremely close comovement shown on this exhibit, without overperformance by the FNC, suggests that the FNC has been less successful than the Major Market in mirroring the movements of the Dow.

Exhibit 3-4 shows the NYSE Composite versus the S&P 500. Recall that the NYSE is very broad based, encompassing all 1600+ stocks listed on the NYSE. The comovement between the two indexes is striking, considering differences in composition and the wide ranging market conditions of the time horizon.

Exhibit 3-5 shows the PHLX National-OTC versus the S&P 500. Recall that the PHLX-OTC is designed to replicate the behavior of the NASDAQ-OTC. This chart reveals the first major deviation from intuitively close comovement between broad-based indexes. The chart demonstrates the relatively poor performance of the small capitalization stocks listed on the NASDAQ during the latter half of the bull market.

Exhibit 3-6 shows the S&P 100 versus the S&P 500. Recall that the S&P 100 is a subset of the S&P 500 comprised of the largest stocks for which options are traded on the CBOE. The comovement between the indexes is good, although a slight spread emerges between them over time. Because the S&P 100 components are selected on the basis of whether their options trade on the CBOE, their relative behavior is not easily explained.

Exhibit 3-7 shows the Value Line Composite versus the S&P 500. Recall that the Value Line is very broad based, encompassing all 1700+ stocks covered by Value Line. This chart reveals that the smaller, second tier stocks contained in the VLC overperformed the S&P 500 over most of the time horizon.

Exhibit 3-8 shows the Dow Jones Industrial Average versus the S&P 500. This chart bears close resemblance to Exhibit 3-2 and its general appearance is explained by the reasons given for that exhibit.

Exhibit 3-9 shows the NASDAQ-OTC versus the S&P 500. This chart bears close resemblance to Exhibit 3-5 and its general appearance is explained by the reasons given for that exhibit.

Exhibit 3-10 shows the Wilshire 5000 versus the S&P 500. Recall that the Wilshire is the broadest of all indexes considered in this book, encompassing some 5000 stocks. The comovement between the indexes is very close, with the Wilshire underperforming during the latter half of the eighties.

CORRELATION ANALYSIS

Correlation analysis is an excellent compliment to charting because it quantifies the intuitive insight obtained through charting. The goal of the analysis is to numerically describe the degree to which two indexes are associated. The analysis does not produce conclusions with respect to causality, meaning that the movement of one index cannot be determined to be dependent upon the movement of another based on correlation analysis. Thus, the analysis is intended solely to describe the strength of association between two indexes.

Correlation Coefficients

The statistic to be used in the correlation analysis is the correlation coefficient. This is a mathematical measure which describes the degree of association between two variables, in this case the returns on market indexes. If the returns on two indexes are perfectly positively correlated such that price movements in one index are exactly matched

EXHIBIT 3-1

AMEX Institutional vs S&P 500

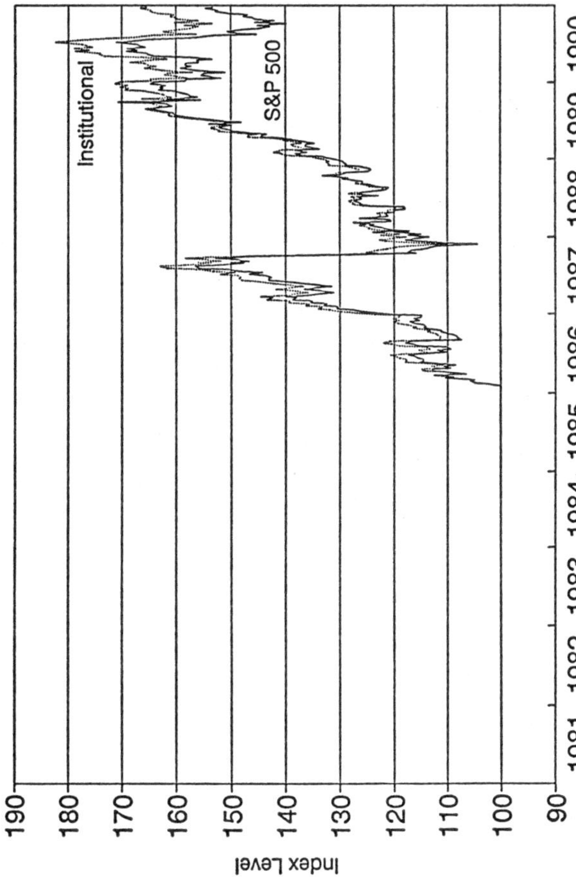

Note: Weekly data normalized to 100 beginning in 1986.

25

EXHIBIT 3-2

AMEX Major Market vs S&P 500

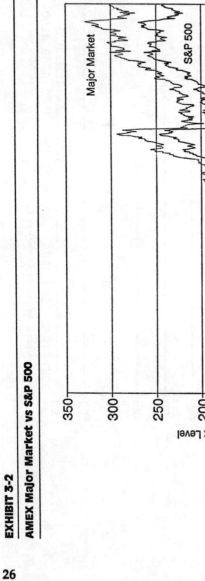

Note: Weekly data normalized to 100 beginning in 1981.

26

EXHIBIT 3-3

Financial News Composite vs S&P 500

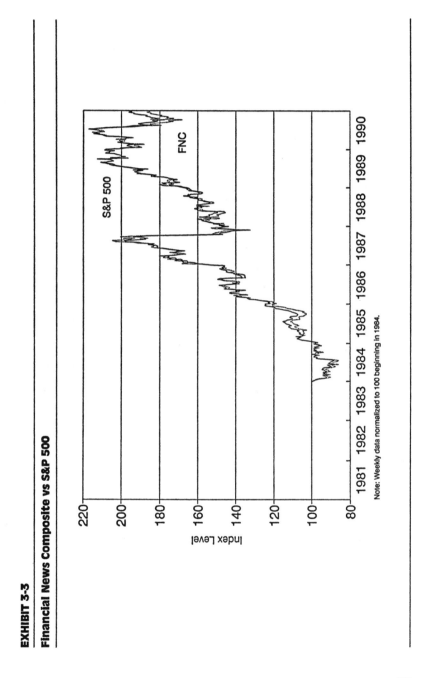

Note: Weekly data normalized to 100 beginning in 1984.

27

EXHIBIT 3-4

NYSE Composite vs S&P 500

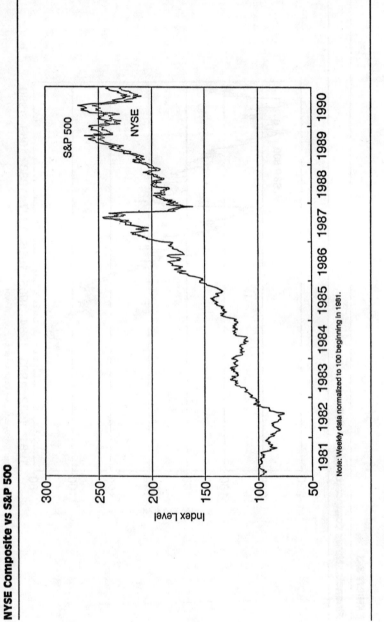

Note: Weekly data normalized to 100 beginning in 1981.

EXHIBIT 3-5

PHLX National-OTC Composite vs S&P 500

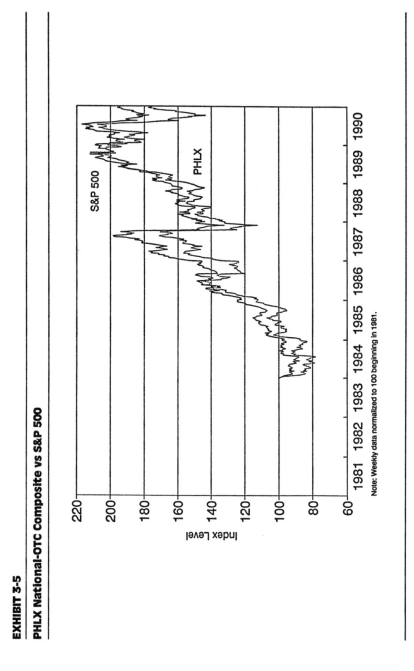

EXHIBIT 3-6

S&P 100 vs S&P 500

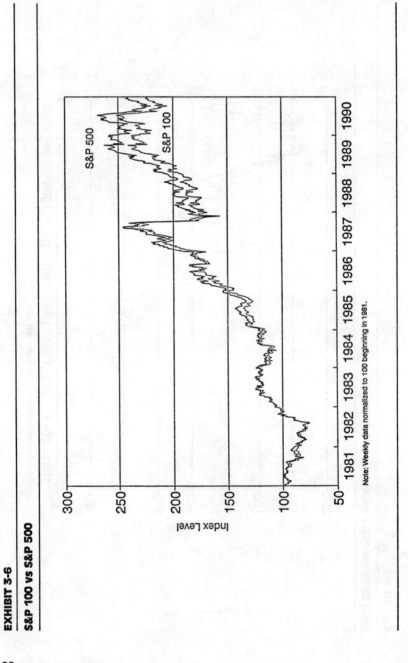

Note: Weekly data normalized to 100 beginning in 1981.

EXHIBIT 3-7

Value Line Composite vs S&P 500

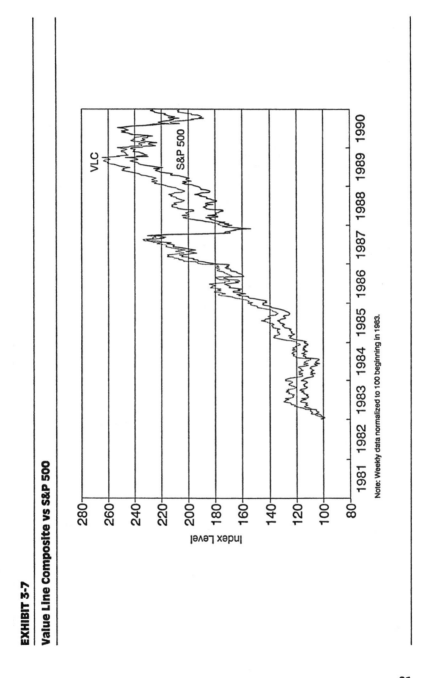

Note: Weekly data normalized to 100 beginning in 1983.

31

EXHIBIT 3-8

Dow Jones Industrial vs S&P 500

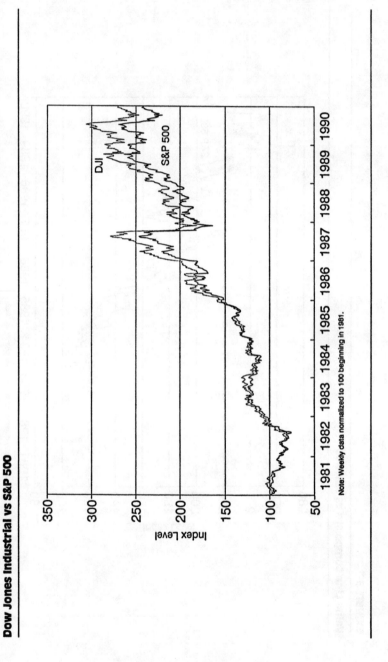

Note: Weekly data normalized to 100 beginning in 1981.

EXHIBIT 3-9

NASDAQ-OTC Composite vs S&P 500

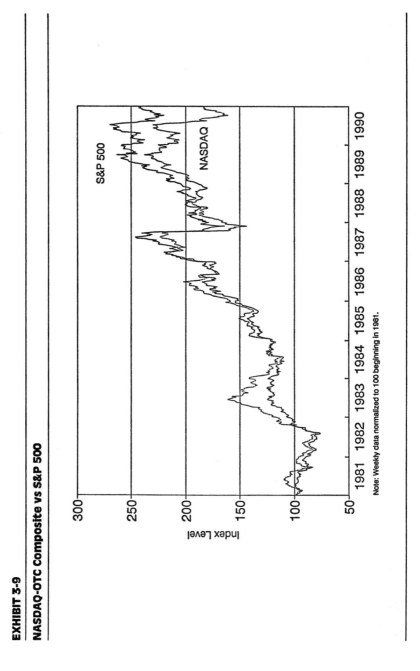

33

34

EXHIBIT 3-10

Wilshire 5000 Equity vs S&P 500

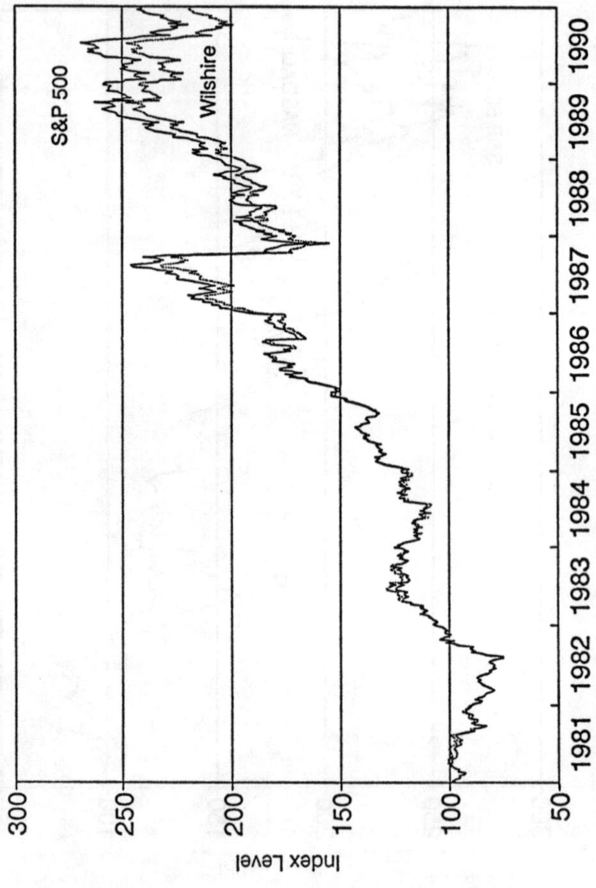

Note: Weekly data normalized to 100 beginning in 1981.

by corresponding movements in the other, the correlation coefficient equals one. If the returns on two indexes are perfectly negatively correlated such that the price movements in one index are exactly matched by corresponding but opposite movements in the other, the correlation coefficient equals negative one. Intermediate degrees of association result in correlation coefficients between one and negative one.

Broad-Based Correlations

Exhibit 3-11 displays the results of a careful correlation analysis process applied to the domestic broad-based indexes charted earlier. The exhibit shows 10–year, 5–year, and 1–year correlations of each index with the S&P 500. For each of the time horizons, the indexes were all positively correlated and generally highly correlated to the S&P 500. This result is expected based on the charting analysis. The results also indicate that correlations are generally stronger over longer time horizons.

Given these differences, investors might wonder which measures should be used in decision making. Although there is no uniformly accepted answer to this question, many people believe that short term

EXHIBIT 3-11

Correlation Coefficients: Index vs S&P 500

	1981-90 10 Year	1986-90 5 Year	1990 1 Year
AMEX Institutional	NA	*0.989	0.941
AMEX Major Market	0.994	0.982	0.906
Financial News Composite	NA	0.991	0.983
NYSE Composite	0.999	0.997	0.993
PHLX National-OTC	NA	0.951	0.964
S&P 100	0.998	0.991	0.990
Value Line Composite	NA	0.924	0.897
Dow Jones Industrial	0.998	0.995	0.979
NASDAQ-OTC Composite	0.960	0.801	0.924
Wilshire 5000 Equity	0.998	0.991	0.982

* data starting 2/7/86

35

EXHIBIT 3-12

Ten-Year Correlation Matrix for Broad-Based Indexes

	AMEX Institutional	AMEX Major Mkt.	Financial News Comp.	NYSE Composite
AMEX Institutional	1.000			
AMEX Major Market	NA	1.000		
Financial News Composite	NA	NA	1.000	
NYSE Composite	NA	0.990	NA	1.000
PHLX National-OTC	NA	NA	NA	NA
S&P 100	NA	0.993	NA	0.998
S&P 500	NA	0.994	NA	0.999
Value Line Composite	NA	NA	NA	NA
Dow Jones Industrial	NA	0.998	NA	0.996
NASDAQ-OTC Composite	NA	0.934	NA	0.968
Wilshire 5000 Equity	NA	0.987	NA	0.999

EXHIBIT 3-13

Five-Year Correlation Matrix for Broad-Based Indexes

	AMEX Institutional*	AMEX Major Mkt.	Financial News Comp.	NYSE Composite
AMEX Institutional	1.000			
AMEX Major Market	0.994	1.000		
Financial News Composite	0.971	0.967	1.000	
NYSE Composite	0.979	0.970	0.993	1.000
PHLX National-OTC	0.907	0.894	0.943	0.954
S&P 100	0.987	0.980	0.987	0.990
S&P 500	0.989	0.982	0.991	0.997
Value Line Composite	0.853	0.853	0.934	0.938
Dow Jones Industrial	0.994	0.993	0.986	0.989
NASDAQ-OTC Composite	0.713	0.693	0.834	0.875
Wilshire 5000 Equity	0.964	0.952	0.991	0.997

* data starting 2/7/91

PHLX Nat.-OTC	S&P 100	S&P 500	Value Line Composite	Dow Jones Industrial	NASDAQ OTC Comp.	Wilshire 5000 Equity
1.000						
NA	1.000					
NA	0.998	1.000				
NA	NA	NA	1.000			
NA	0.997	0.998	NA	1.000		
NA	0.963	0.960	NA	0.951	1.000	
NA	0.997	0.998	NA	0.994	0.975	1.000

PHLX Nat.-OTC	S&P 100	S&P 500	Value Line Composite	Dow Jones Industrial	NASDAQ OTC Comp.	Wilshire 5000 Equity
1.000						
0.916	1.000					
0.951	0.991	1.000				
0.961	0.894	0.924	1.000			
0.923	0.993	0.995	0.897	1.000		
0.860	0.797	0.801	0.895	0.767	1.000	
0.963	0.983	0.991	0.951	0.979	0.871	1.000

EXHIBIT 3-14

One-Year Correlation Matrix for Broad-Based Indexes

	AMEX Institutional	AMEX Major Mkt.	Financial News Comp.	NYSE Composite
AMEX Institutional	1.000			
AMEX Major Market	0.987	1.000		
Financial News Composite	0.898	0.850	1.000	
NYSE Composite	0.913	0.873	0.991	1.000
PHLX National-OTC	0.838	0.792	0.970	0.980
S&P 100	0.965	0.933	0.980	0.982
S&P 500	0.941	0.906	0.983	0.993
Value Line Composite	0.715	0.654	0.942	0.933
Dow Jones Industrial	0.963	0.943	0.967	0.971
NASDAQ-OTC Composite	0.760	0.701	0.961	0.952
Wilshire 5000 Equity	0.877	0.830	0.992	0.996

historical correlations are more appropriate for short term investment programs, while longer term correlations should be used for longer term investment programs. Thus, an investor using options positions for a strategy of less then one year might use one-year correlations, while an investor embarking on a sustained multi-year strategy of successive index options positions might use five- or ten-year historical correlations.

In the interest of completeness, Exhibits 3-12 through 3-14 show the correlation of each index with every other index for the ten-, five-, and one-year time horizons respectively.

PRACTICAL IMPLICATIONS

The primary conclusion of the foregoing analyses is that with the possible exception of over-the-counter stocks, broad-based index movements are positive and highly correlated. Conservatively, one might say that the selection of any broad-based index option is likely to

PHLX Nat.-OTC	S&P 100	S&P 500	Value Line Composite	Dow Jones Industrial	NASDAQ OTC Comp.	Wilshire 5000 Equity
1.000						
0.937	1.000					
0.964	0.990	1.000				
0.957	0.867	0.897	1.000			
0.918	0.991	0.979	0.856	1.000		
0.972	0.898	0.924	0.996	0.887	1.000	
0.988	0.967	0.982	0.961	0.955	0.975	1.000

produce a result which is at least in the same direction as any other. A more liberal interpretation supposes that the result achieved through random index option selection may be extremely close to that achieved through a more careful selection process. While it appears in this case that the markets are somewhat forgiving of investor carelessness, a careful index option selection process is nonetheless highly recommended.

The recommended approach to index option selection requires primary attention to the elements discussed in Chapters 2 & 3: index construction and historical index price movements.

1. Investors should make every effort to choose an index with construction characteristics which most closely represent those associated with the desired market exposure.

2. Investors should make every effort to choose an index with the highest possible historical correlation to the desired market exposure.

It should be understood that neither similar construction nor historically high correlations guarantee that the performance of the index will mirror that of the desired market. However, absent clairvoyance, they are theoretically sound principles upon which selection decisions can be rationally based.

LOOKING AHEAD

This concludes the discussion of the theory and implications of index construction methods. Chapters 2 and 3 provided the investor with insight regarding the movement of indexes underlying stock index options. Given this perspective, the discussion now turns to the nature of index options themselves.

4

Index Options

Any intelligent discussion of options is necessarily involved. It must navigate through puts and calls, buyers and writers, premiums, contract multipliers, and a host of other specialized terminology peculiar to options trading. This chapter is a brief but thorough introduction to this complex and specialized world. No prior knowledge of options theory is assumed. Because the focus of the discussion is index (rather than stock) options, ideas which are common to both types of options are presented in terms of index options. Concepts unique to index options are clearly marked. The scope of the discussion is limited to information that is of the greatest practical value. For more detailed discussions of options and options theory, the reader is referred to the bibliography at the end of this book.

In many respects stock index options are identical to listed stock options. They are traded in a similar manner on the major exchanges and employ many of the same concepts and principles. Most option based investment strategies can be implemented using either option type. Therefore, an understanding of one implies a basic understanding of the other. Despite these similarities, however, there are certain differences between index options and stock options that are significant. These differences are important because they impact investment risk and performance. This chapter first reviews general principles of options, then outlines the important differences between index options and stock options. An understanding of general principles of options and the unique features of index options will set the stage for the discussion of index options strategies in Chapter 5.

GENERAL PRINCIPLES

Many principles of options theory apply to both stock options and index options. The following discussion reviews these general principles in terms of index options. Readers familiar with the general principles of options theory may wish to skip this discussion and move directly to the next section on the unique features of index options.

Call Options

A call option is the right, but not the obligation, to **buy** a *specific amount* of a *specific security*, at a *specific price*, on or before a *specific date*. The four variables highlighted in this definition comprise the most important features of any options contract.

The *specific security* in an index option contract is the underlying index. This means that the index is treated as though it were a stock that can be bought or sold. For example, the S&P 500 index recently closed at about 311. Therefore, the investor can think of the index as a stock with a share price of $311.

The *specific amount* of security in an index option contract is called the contract multiplier. This is simply the number of shares of index that can be bought. The contract multiplier for all index option contracts is standardized at 100. Therefore, the holder of a call on an index has the right to buy 100 shares of the index .

The *specific price* at which the holder of an index call option can buy shares is called the exercise price or strike price. For example, consider an S&P 500 call option with a strike price of $325. An investor holding such an option would have the right to purchase 100 shares of S&P 500 at $325 per share. If the index rises to 330, the investor earns $500 because the value of each share has increased $5 beyond the strike. The investor's net earnings would equal the $500 less the amount paid to acquire the option.

The *specific date* at or before which an option may be exercised is called the maturity date or expiration date. (Certain index option contracts can only be exercised on the maturity date—not before it—and investors should familiarize themselves with the exercise style of any specific option prior to trading it. Exercise styles are discussed in more detail later in this chapter.) Maturity dates for all index options are standardized at the Saturday following the third Friday of each month. For example, the holder of a September call must exercise or sell the option by the close of business on the third Friday of September, otherwise the option will expire on the following day. If the index level does not rise above the strike price by the expiration date, the call option expires worthless.

Consider Exhibit 4-1 which displays a reprint of S&P 500 options quotes from *The New York Times* on August 25, 1990. Notice how the four definitive variables are (or aren't) specified. The **underlying security** is the S&P 500 Index and is clearly listed at the top of all quotes. The **strike price** is also clearly marked for each quote. The **date**

EXHIBIT 4-1

S. & P. 500 (CBOE)

Option & Strike NY Close Price	Calls-Last Sep	Oct	Nov	Puts-Last Sep	Oct	Nov
SP500 250	62⅝	r	s	¾	1⅞	s
311.51 275	39½	s	s	2⅜	s	s
311.51 300	18	r	s	6⅜	10⅝	s
311.51 305	14⅝	r	s	7¾	12	s
311.51 310	11	15½	s	9⅜	13¼	s
311.51 315	8⅝	13¼	s	11	17	s
311.51 320	5⅞	9⅜	s	14	18	s
311.51 325	4	7¼	s	16¾	20⅝	s
311.51 330	2⁵⁄₁₆	5⅜	s	19¾	24½	s
311.51 335	1⅜	4	s	25½	30	s
311.51 340	¾	3	s	33⅜	r	s
311.51 345	⁷⁄₁₆	1¾	s	34	r	s
311.51 350	⅜	r	s	42⅝	r	s
311.51 355	¼	⅞	s	48	r	s
311.51 360	³⁄₁₆	½	s	49¾	r	s
311.51 370	r	s	s	58½	s	s
311.51 375	¹⁄₁₆	s	s	62⅜	s	s

Total Call Vol.25,171 Call Open Int.334,377
Total Put Vol.42,671 Put Open Int.510,958

43

of expiration is shown only as an expiration *month*, and investors are assumed to know that the actual *date* is the Saturday following the third Friday of the month. Finally, the **amount of underlying security** is not specified at all; thus, investors must be familiar with this contract to know the correct multiplier is 100.

Now consider other information of interest in Exhibit 4-1. Note that the prior day's closing index level is shown as 311.51. Also, note that the prices of options are expressed as the dollar price divided by the contract multiplier. Thus, while the September 325 call (mentioned above) is quoted in the exhibit at price of 4, it actually costs 4 times 100 (the contract multiplier) or $400. This price is also known as the option *premium*. The daily trading volume is shown underneath the quotes and is expressed as contracts traded. The open interest number indicates the number of outstanding contracts on the exchange. As people enter into new contracts, open interest expands. As people exercise existing contracts, or as existing contracts expire, open interest declines. The word "last" appears after Puts and Calls to indicate that the prices shown are the last executed prices of the trading day.

Continuing with the the S&P 500 September 325 call from Exhibit 4-1, Exhibit 4-2 displays the possible dollar profits of this call at the end of trading on the third Friday in September. The value of the option at this time is called the *expiration value* and the set of profit possibilities is called the *expiration profit profile*. The expiration value and expiration profit both depend upon the level of the underlying index, however they are not the same. If the index is below the strike at expiration, the option expires worthless (expiration value equals zero) and the investor loses the cost of the option (expiration profit equals – $400). *Thus, the expiration profit is the set of profit and loss opportunities that arise at expiration as a result of the investment position.* As the index level rises above the strike, the option becomes increasingly valuable. If the index trades to a level of 330, the expiration profit is $100. At this level, expiration value equals $500. The investor recovers the $400 premium plus earns a profit of $100. The breakeven point— the index level at which expiration value exactly equals the cost of the option— is 329.

EXHIBIT 4-2

Expiration Profile of an S&P 500 September 325 Call

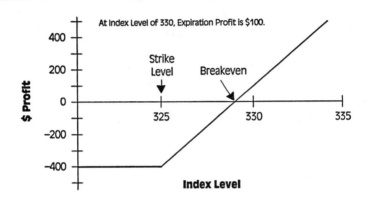

Put Options

A put option is the right, but not the obligation, to **sell** a *specific amount* of a *specific security*, at a *specific price*, on or before a *specific date*. Notice that the definition for a put is identical to that for a call except the word **buy** has been replaced with the word **sell**.

Returning to Exhibit 4-1, consider the S&P 500 October 305 put option. The cost of this option is quoted at 12, meaning 12 times 100 or $1200. An investor holding such an option would have the right to sell 100 shares of S&P 500 at $305 per share. If the index falls to 300, the investor earns $500 because the value of each share has decreased $5 beyond the strike. The investor's net earnings would equal the $500 less the amount paid to acquire the option. (Therefore, at an index level of 300 net earnings to the investor would be a $700 loss!) The breakeven point is an index level 12 points lower than the strike, or 293. Since the index is currently trading at 311, the investor breaks even if the index drops by 18 points prior to expiration.

Exhibit 4-3 displays the possible expiration dollar profits of this put. As with the call, both the expiration value and expiration profit depend directly upon the level of the underlying index. If the index

45

level is above the strike price at expiration, the option expires worthless and the investor loses the cost of the option—$1200. As the index level falls below the strike, the option becomes increasingly valuable. If the index trades to a level of 293, the profit of the option is zero because the value of the option is $1200, exactly offsetting its initial cost.

With the index currently trading at 311, the put and the call options discussed above are both 18 points away from breakeven. The call breaks even at 329, while the put breaks even at 293. Despite this seeming equality, the put costs three times more than the call. Several intuitive explanations can account for the discrepancy. First, the put, which expires in October, has twice as long to maturity as the call, which expires in September. A longer option is always worth more than a shorter option because it extends the time frame during which the underlying index may move to the benefit of the holder. Second, a bearish sentiment in the marketplace prevailed at the time due to tensions in the Middle East. Therefore, options that profited from downward moves in the market were more expensive than those that profited from upward moves.

EXHIBIT 4-3

Expiration Profile of an S&P 500 October 305 Put

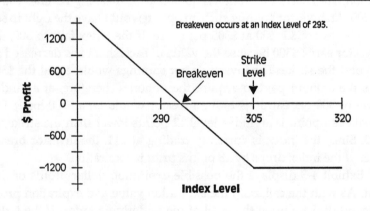

Exercise Styles

The exercise styles associated with options can be classified into two major categories: American and European. American exercise means that the option can be exercised by the holder at any time during its life. European exercise means that the option can be exercised by the holder only at expiration. Either option type can be bought or sold at any time during its life. Although at expiration the exercise style is irrelevant,the exercise style prior to expiration may have a material impact upon the value of the option and the action of the holder (as discussed in Chapter 6). For these reasons, investors should be familiar with the exercise procedure associated with any stock index option prior to trading it. Exercise styles are detailed in the contract specifications for each index option (see Appendix C).

Matched Transactions

To this point only the *holders* of index options have been considered. Recall that the holder of a call (or put) holds the right, but not the obligation, to buy (or sell) a specific amount of a specific stock at a specific price on or before a specific date. One might reasonably wonder who stands on the opposite side of an options transaction, ready to trade with the option holder upon demand. The other party is the option *writer*, the person who receives the option premium as consideration for agreeing to perform on the other side of the options contract. The holder and the writer are essentially making a bet, with the exchange functioning as a matchmaker. In consideration for matching buyers with sellers, the exchange receives a commission. This fact reveals one of the more sobering aspects of options trading: that every transaction has a winner and a loser. Options are not wealth generating assets like stocks. Rather, they are redistributive vehicles which merely transfer wealth between people.

UNIQUE FEATURES

During the discussion of general principles, newcomers to index options were encouraged to think in terms of buying and selling "shares" of an underlying index. Because underlying indexes are

47

treated exactly like underlying stocks in options markets, this analogy remains a useful conceptual tool. However, investors must understand, in no uncertain terms, that indexes are in reality composite measures for which no actual shares exist. In fact, the most important feature separating index options from stock options is that *shares of underlying indexes cannot be bought or sold as can shares of underlying stock*. This unique feature of index options leads to a variety of special risks and circumstances for participants in the index options markets.

Basis Risk

Basis risk is a factor for index option participants (but not for stock option participants) that arises because shares of the underlying index cannot actually be bought or sold. Consider the writer of a stock call option. This writer may arrange in advance for settlement of such a contract by acquiring underlying stock sufficient for settlement at the outset of the contract. This protects the writer against potentially large losses, and is known as *covered* call writing.

For example, assume the writer of an IBM September 120 call (contract multiplier = 100) purchases the stock for $120 and charges $200 as the option in premium. Upon exercise with the stock at $125, the writer would be required to sell to the holder the stock at $120 per share. The net result to the writer is a $200 gain. (The writer's stock purchase and sale transactions wash, and the option premium earned is $200.) Had the call not been covered, known as writing a *naked* call, the writer would be required to purchase the stock in the open market for $125 at exercise, then sell it back to the holder at $120. The net result is a $300 loss. (The writer's stock purchase and sale transactions cost the writer $500 but the $200 earned in premium partially offsets that cost.) Thus, covered call writing means that the writer has acquired underlying stock sufficient for settlement in advance of the actual settlement date.

Covering call options protects writers because the underlying stock provides a hedge against market value changes over the life of the option. Regardless of how high the market goes, the covered writer can always deliver the underlying stock that was purchased in advance at lower levels. Unfortunately, perfectly covered call writing is impossible with stock index options because shares of the index cannot be purchased in advance to satisfy settlement requirements. An index call writer can achieve partial protection by holding a portfolio of securities that are representative of the index; however, such a portfolio can be expected only to approximate the market value changes of the index. To the extent that the price movement of such a portfolio varies from the price movement of the index, a spread (or basis) emerges between the value of the portfolio and the value of the index. Therefore, writers of call options covered in this way accept an unavoidable measure of basis risk.

Cash Settlement

Although writers can substantially cover index call options by holding a portfolio of securities that represent the index, shares of this portfolio are not deliverable to the holder upon exercise as are shares of stock underlying a stock option. Therefore, unlike stock options which can be settled either with cash or underlying stock, index options must be settled in cash. For instance, in the above example the writer might deliver IBM stock at $120 per share (stock settlement) or simply pay the holder $500 (cash settlement). In contrast, because indexes are composite measures for which no deliverable shares of stock exist, stock settlement is not an alternative and cash settlement is required. Although it is not a risk, cash settlement is a consequence of the fact that shares of underlying indexes cannot be bought or sold.

Timing Risk

Timing risk is another risk type which arises from the fact that shares of underlying indexes cannot be bought or sold. Consider the writer of an index call. When the option holder exercises, the writer is said to be "assigned". Although the exchange market will notify the writer of assignment as soon as possible, writers are generally not aware of assignment until the business day following exercise at earliest. This time lag between exercise and notification of assignment occurs generally in the options markets; however, it is problematic only for index options participants because it is impossible for the

49

latter to acquire shares of the underlying index which are deliverable at settlement.

Assume the holder of an AMEX Major Market 555 call (recall that contract multiplier = 100 for all index options) exercises at a closing index level of 560. The holder is thus due $500. To hedge the call, the writer purchased a portfolio of stocks designed to duplicate the price movement of the Major Market Index when the index level was 555. If the writer knows immediately of assignment, the portfolio is sold upon exercise at a market value corresponding to an index level of 560 and the $500 cash settlement is fully funded from the proceeds. However, consider what happens if, by the time the writer is notified of assignment, the Major Market (and hence the value of the hedge portfolio) has fallen by 10 points. The writer must now sell the portfolio in the open market at value corresponding to an index level of 550. The $500 cash settlement to the holder is still due, but the proceeds from the sale of the portfolio will not fund it. The writer has lost $1000 in proceeds from the sale of the portfolio due to timing risk.

Note that stock options writers need only deliver securities instead of cash to avoid the impact of timing risk. If the securities have declined in value between exercise and delivery, this loss of value is borne by the holder. However, because cash settlement is required, writers of index options must convert hedge portfolios to cash upon notification of assignment and bear the risk that the value of the index has changed since exercise.

Exercise Risk

Exercise risk is distinct from the other unique risks discussed because it is unrelated to the fact that shares of underlying indexes cannot be bought or sold. Exercise risk arises from the fact that the exercise of an index option is recognized by the exchange market only *at the close*. An investor wishing to exercise during midday must recognize that the value of the option may be very different by the day's end when the exchange will recognize the exercise and determine option value.

Assume the holder of a NYSE Composite September 180 call decides to exercise during morning trading at about 10:00 am when the index level is 185. In theory, the holder is due $500. However, consider what happens if, by the time the market closes, the index level has fallen to 175. Although the holder exercised at 10:00 am, the index level used to calculate the option value is the level at the close. In this case the holder actually loses $500 and must pay that amount to the writer in cash at settlement! As this example makes clear, holders of index options should always exercise late in the day to minimize the impact of exercise risk. Another alternative is to simply sell the option rather than exercise it because the sale can occur at midday index levels.

PRACTICAL IMPLICATIONS

The foregoing discussion suggests that the subtleties and unique risks of index options trading are significant. However, individual investors should not be discouraged by these complexities. Importantly, the discussion reveals that these risks are of greater concern to writers than holders. For example, only writers must decide whether they will trade covered or uncovered options. Covered writers must next consider the potential impact of unique risks such as basis risk and timing risk. Basis risk can be minimized by constructing an effective hedge portfolio; however, timing risk is difficult to reduce. Neither can be completely eliminated.

The burden of analysis and expertise appears to be less for holders. The primary unique risk to holders is exercise risk, which can be effectively managed by exercising near the close or selling rather than exercising. Holders are also subject to basis risk when hedging; however, this can be managed through good index selection and/or good portfolio construction. While all this does suggest that buying options requires less expertise than selling them, it does not suggest that buyers of index options should be less earnest than sellers in their preparation to invest in these vehicles. Both groups are subject to and should be familiar with the risk and reward profiles related to a specific transaction. Both groups should keep foremost in their minds that options trading is a zero sum game: there is always a winner and a loser. Both groups should take great care in design and implementation of index option investment strategies.

LOOKING AHEAD

This concludes the basic examination of options. The reader should note well the expiration profit profiles shown for the long call (Exhibit 4-2) and long put (Exhibit 4-3) positions. Chapter 5 will focus on strategies that combine options with stock positions and/or other options using the profit profiles as strategic building blocks.

5

Index Option Strategies

The holder of an option assumes a unique expiration profit profile. Implicit in that notion is the corollary that the *writer* of the option assumes an equal but opposite profile at expiration. These profiles are useful conceptual tools for understanding options theory. Interestingly, profit profiles can be extended to common stock theory. Long or short positions in common stock also constitute unique profit profiles to investors, though no expiration dates are attached. Both long and short investors in common stock assume profits that match the movement of the stock price one for one. The generalized profit profiles for options and stock investors are displayed in Exhibit 5-1. These profiles are the building blocks of options strategy.

Countless viable investment strategies can be created using the building blocks shown in Exhibit 5-1. This is because the combinations that are possible using varying amounts of calls, puts, and common stocks are literally endless. Each combination produces a unique (and to some investor somewhere, desirable) profile of expiration values, and the goal of every option strategy is to create a desired profit profile. In fact, classical options theory suggests that any feasible expiration profile can be created by combining the appropriate options and securities positions, though in reality the required positions

EXHIBIT 5-1

Generalized Payoffs for Stock and Options Investors

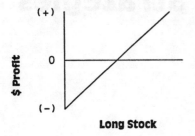

Long Stock

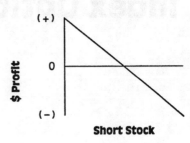

Short Stock

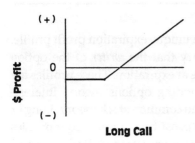

Long Call

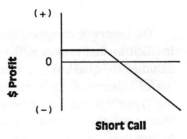

Short Call

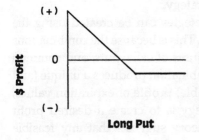

Long Put

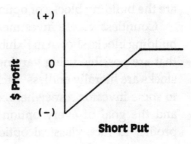

Short Put

may not be practically available to investors. Combination strategies can become quite complex. This chapter concentrates on classic combinations that are most frequently utilized in the marketplace.

HEDGING

Hedging strategies are defensive mechanisms for controlling and reducing net investment risk. They involve index option positions in conjunction with common stock and are intended to nullify a portion of market exposure associated with the stock by assuming an equal but opposite market exposure with options. As emphasized earlier, successful hedging through index options will depend largely upon the degree to which the movement of the underlying index corresponds to the movement of the securities being hedged.

Protective Puts

Probably the most common method for defending a portfolio against market decline is the purchase of put options whose value will increase as the market falls. If the puts are perfectly matched to the portfolio, their increase in value will be exactly offset by the decrease in value of the portfolio. In this way, the investor avoids the portfolio loss associated with a declining market while retaining the original holdings. On the upside, however, the purchase of protective put options have little impact. Investors implementing this strategy in a rising market enjoy the appreciation of their portfolios less the cost of the put options.

Consider an investor holding shares in an S&P 500 indexed mutual fund with a total market value of $62,000 on August 24, 1990. Iraq had invaded Kuwait earlier in the month causing an equity market downturn, and the investor fears further market decline. Specifically, the investor believes that if shooting occurs in the Gulf the market will drop substantially. On the other hand, if a negotiated settlement is reached the market will likely rebound. The investor has considered liquidating the portfolio but is reluctant to do so for several reasons. Liquidation would eliminate the upside potential associated with negotiated settlement, generate unpleasant transactions costs, and be

55

EXHIBIT 5-2

S. & P. 500 (CBOE)

Option & Strike NY Close Price		Calls-Last			Puts-Last		
		Sep	Oct	Nov	Sep	Oct	Nov
SP500	250	62⅝	r	s	¾	1⅞	s
311.51	275	39½	s	s	2⅜	s	s
311.51	300	18	r	s	6⅜	10⅝	s
311.51	305	14⅝	r	s	7¾	12	s
311.51	310	11	15½	s	9⅜	13¼	s
311.51	315	8⅝	13¼	s	11	17	s
311.51	320	5⅞	9⅜	s	14	18	s
311.51	325	4	7¼	s	16¾	20⅝	s
311.51	330	2⁵/₁₆	5⅜	s	19¾	24½	s
311.51	335	1⅜	4	s	25½	30	s
311.51	340	¾	3	s	33⅜	r	s
311.51	345	⁷/₁₆	1¾	s	34	r	s
311.51	350	⅜	r	s	42⅝	r	s
311.51	355	¼	⅞	s	48	r	s
311.51	360	³/₁₆	½	s	49¾	r	s
311.51	370	r	s	s	58½	s	s
311.51	375	¹/₁₆	s	s	62⅜	s	s

Total Call Vol.25,171 Call Open Int.334,377
Total Put Vol.42,671 Put Open Int.510,958

inconsistent with the investor's long term view. Therefore, the investor decides to purchase put options to temporarily hedge the downside exposure of the equity holdings.

Because the investor's mutual fund portfolio is specifically constructed to track the performance of the S&P 500, the investor realizes that options on the S&P 500 are likely to provide an excellent hedge. Exhibit 5-2 displays again the S&P 500 options quotes for August 25, 1990 (first shown in Chapter 4) and shows a closing index level of 311.51. The investor believes that the next eight weeks will be crucial to the outcome of the crises and therefore chooses the October contract. The investor is only interested in protecting against further market decline and therefore decides on a strike price about equal to current market levels. The exhibit shows the price of an S&P 500 October 310 put (which provides roughly eight weeks of protection) is 13.25 or $1325.

The investor now faces an important question with a simple but not obvious answer: how many puts are required to hedge the portfolio? When employing index options, the number of options required should be computed irrespective of the strike chosen. Thus, the correct methodology is to divide portfolio value by the index level x 100. The investor with a $62,000 portfolio should purchase 62,000/ 31,151 = 2 (rounded) put options to correctly hedge the portfolio. At $1325 per option, the cost of the hedge is $2650 before transactions costs. Commissions at a discount broker should be about 2% of the cost of the options but are ignored throughout this chapter to simplify the presentation. Commissions are discussed in more detail in Chapter 9. The investor buys the options.

Exhibit 5-3 displays the net expiration profit profile which the investor has created through the combination of two strategic building blocks: long stock and long put options. The investor can expect this net profile to prevail on the third Friday in October 1990 roughly eight weeks in the future. Notice that the net profile is derived by combining the expiration profiles of the two component building blocks. (That is, each point on the net profile equals the sum of the two corresponding points on the component profiles.) The exhibit shows that if the market remains above the strike, the options will expire worthless and the net profit will equal the expiration profit of the stock portfolio less the cost of the options. If the market falls below the strike, the options will increase in value by an amount which offsets the loss in value of the stocks.

Exhibit 5-3 shows that the investor's profit at expiration depends directly upon the level of the underlying index because both the option value and the portfolio value move in lock step with the index. Had the stock portfolio been less well matched with the index, the investor would have experienced some drift (positive or negative) in the profit shown due to basis risk. The exhibit also shows that the protective put strategy is essentially an insurance policy against a falling market. The effect of the hedge is to maintain the net investment roughly at the starting portfolio value (less the cost of the options) regardless of how low the market goes. Finally, it is interesting to note that the net profile looks very much like the generalized profile for a long call option. In fact, the investor has created what is known as a *synthetic* call on the S&P 500, a concept discussed in more detail in

EXHIBIT 5-3

Protective Put Example

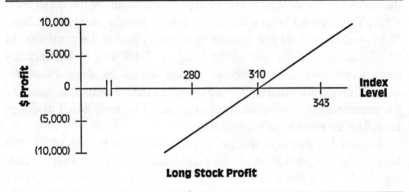

Long Stock Profit

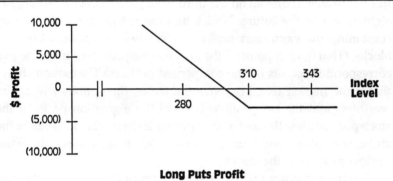

Long Puts Profit

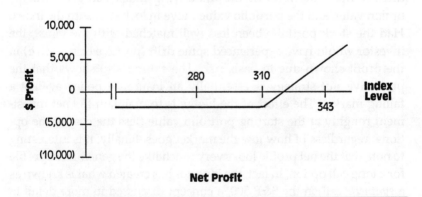

Net Profit

EXHIBIT 5-4

Protective Put Example: Calculation of Expiration Profit Profile

Initial Security Statistics

Index Level	311.51
Portfolio Value	$62,000
Strategy	Buy 2 SPX Oct 310 puts @ 13 1/4 = $2650

Expiration Profit Profile

Index Change	-10%	-5%	0%	5%	10%
Index Level	280.36	295.93	311.51	327.09	342.66
Portfolio Value	$55,800	$58,900	$62,000	$65,100	$68,200
Portfolio Profit	($6,200)	($3,100)	$0	$3,100	$6,200
Puts Value	$5,928	$2,813	$0	$0	$0
Puts Profit	$3,278	$163	($2,650)	($2,650)	($2,650)
Net Profit	($2,922)	($2,937)	($2,650)	$450	$3,550

Chapter 8. Exhibit 5-4 summarizes the hedge numerically and displays the results of discrete market moves.

Finally, note that the cost of the hedge is significant at about 4.3% of starting portfolio value. The high cost in this example reflects the tendency of index put options to become relatively expensive after a major market pullback as occurred during August 1990.

Covered Call Writing

As discussed in Chapter 4, perfectly covered call writing is impossible with stock index options because shares of the index cannot be purchased in advance to satisfy settlement requirements. However, an index call writer can achieve partial protection by holding a portfolio which is representative of the index. To the extent that the price movement of such a portfolio varies from the price movement of the index, the investor encounters basis risk. Basis risk notwithstanding, there are times when it makes sense for an investor in common stocks to write index call options against a diversified portfolio. The objective of such a strategy is to earn additional money in the form of captured option premiums.

59

EXHIBIT 5-5

New York

N.Y.S.E. Composite Index

Option & Strike NY Close	Price	Calls-Last Sep	Calls-Last Oct	Calls-Last Nov	Puts-Last Sep	Puts-Last Oct	Puts-Last Nov
NY Idx	155	r	r	r	2 1/4	3 3/8	r
171.05	160	r	r	r	3 1/8	4 1/2	r
171.05	165	r	r	r	3 3/8	5 1/2	r
171.05	170	4 5/8	r	s	5 3/4	7 1/2	s
171.05	175	3 1/4	r	r	7 1/8	8 3/4	r
171.05	177 1/2	1 3/4	r	s	r	r	s
171.05	180	1 3/16	3	r	11 1/2	13 5/8	r
171.05	182 1/2	r	r	s	14 5/8	14 1/4	s
171.05	185	3/8	1 7/8	r	14	15 7/8	r
171.05	190	1/4	r	r	r	r	r
171.05	192 1/2	r	s	s	23	s	s

Total Call Vol. 793 Call Open Int. 8,887
Total Put Vol. 369 Put Open Int. 1,986

Consider an investor holding a well diversified portfolio of common stocks that trade predominantly on the New York Stock Exchange and are worth $52,500 on August 25, 1990. Because of the trouble in the Persian Gulf, the investor believes that the market has little upside potential. Specifically, the investor perceives the situation as stalemated between a belligerent Iraq which refuses to withdraw from Kuwait, and a unified international community which is determined to see pre-invasion conditions restored. Until the crises is resolved, the investor believes the markets cannot move significantly upward. Therefore, the investor decides to sell (temporarily) the upside potential of the portfolio by writing index call options that will hedge the upside exposure of the equity holdings.

After a careful examination of the composition and construction of the portfolio relative to the available optionable indexes, the investor determines that the options on the NYSE Composite index are probably the best fit for the strategy. Exhibit 5-5 displays the NYSE Composite options quotes for August 24, 1990 and shows a closing index level of 171.05. The investor believes that the upcoming four week period is a time horizon over which no favorable resolution of the conflict will occur and therefore chooses the September contract. However, the investor believes the market could move slightly upward during the time horizon and therefore decides on a strike price slightly above current market levels. The exhibit shows the price of a NYSE Composite September 175 call is 3.25 or $325.

The investor must now determine how many calls will correctly hedge the portfolio. Using the methodology from the previous example, the correct number of options is 52,500/17,105 = 3 (rounded). At $325 per option, the income captured from the hedge is $975. The investor sells the options.

Exhibit 5-6 displays the net expiration profit profile that the investor has created through the combination of two strategic building blocks: long stock and short call options. The investor can expect this net profile to prevail on the third Friday in September 1990 roughly four weeks in the future. Notice again that the net profile is derived by combining the expiration profiles of the two components. This method of combining individual profiles to determine a net profile works in all cases and with any number of components. The exhibit shows that if the market remains below the strike, the options will expire worthless and the net profit will equal the expiration profit of the stock portfolio plus the option premiums captured. If the market rises above the strike, the loss in options value (which must be paid to the holder at expiration) will be offset by the rise in value of the underlying portfolio.

The dominant feature of the covered call hedge is that the investor has traded away the upside of the portfolio for option premium. The hedge turns out to be a good decision if the market maintains current levels or moves downward. Again, the net profit at expiration is shown to depend directly on the movement of the index because the example assumes perfect correlation between the index and the underlying portfolio. Basis risk will cause some deviation in expected return. Finally, it is interesting to note that the net profile looks very much like the generalized profile for a short put option. In fact, this strategy equates to a synthetic short put on the NYSE Composite

EXHIBIT 5-6

Covered Call Example

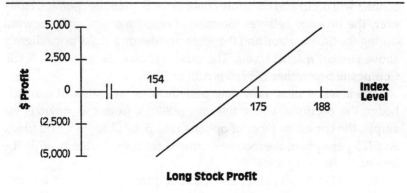

Long Stock Profit

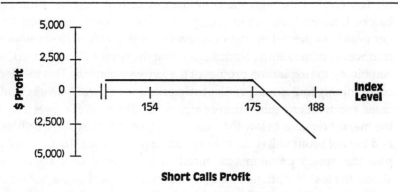

Short Calls Profit

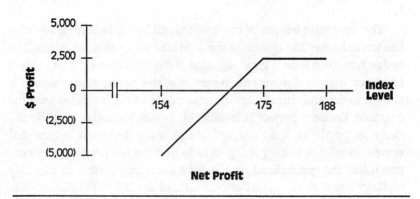

Net Profit

EXHIBIT 5-7

Covered Call Example: Calculation of Expiration Profit Profile

Initial Security Statistics

Index Level	171.05
Portfolio Value	$52,500
Strategy	Sell 3 NYA Sep 175 calls @ 3 1/4 = $975

Expiration Profit Profile

Index Change	−10%	−5%	0%	5%	10%
Index Level	153.95	162.50	171.05	179.60	188.16
Portfolio Value	$47,250	$49,875	$52,500	$55,125	$57,750
Portfolio Profit	($5,250)	($2,625)	$0	$2,625	$5,250
Calls Value	$0	$0	$0	($1,381)	($3,947)
Calls Profit	$975	$975	$975	($406)	($2,972)
Net Profit	($4,275)	($1,650)	$975	$2,219	$2,279

Index. Exhibit 5-7 summarizes the hedge numerically and displays the results of discrete market moves.

During the eighties, mutual funds were introduced which use covered call writing (on individual stocks) as a regular source of additional investment income. The percieved advantages of covered call writing resulted in about $7 billion committed to these funds by 1988. However, option income funds (which typically hold a well diversified collection of good quality stocks) have consistently lagged the S&P 500 index on a total return basis, evidencing the weakness of covered call writing as an ongoing portfolio strategy. In addition, covered call writing generates strong income streams that are undesirable to tax sensitive investors.

Blended Calls

As a final hedging strategy example, consider an investor holding a small portfolio of blue chip industrial stocks that all trade on the NYSE and are worth $54,250 on August 24, 1990. Like the investor in the covered call example, this investor perceived the small probability

EXHIBIT 5-8

American

Major Market Index

Option & NY Close	Strike Price	Calls-Last Sep	Calls-Last Oct	Calls-Last Nov	Puts-Last Sep	Puts-Last Oct	Puts-Last Nov
MMIdx	460	r	r	r	4¾	9¼	r
514.96	470	44¾	r	r	6	10⅞	r
514.96	480	36¾	r	r	7½	12½	18⅛
514.96	490	r	r	r	9⅞	15¾	20⅝
514.96	500	27⅝	r	34	11½	18¼	23½
514.96	505	23¾	30	r	13	23½	r
514.96	510	20¼	28⅝	r	14¾	22¾	26⅞
514.96	515	14	22½	r	16⅝	25⅜	r
514.96	520	15	r	r	18¾	29⅜	30⅞
514.96	525	12½	20	r	21¼	29	r
514.96	530	10	15⅝	r	23⅝	27¾	r
514.96	535	7⅝	13⅝	r	25½	r	r
514.96	540	6¼	9⅜	r	28½	35⅛	40⅝
514.96	545	4⅝	8⅛	r	33¼	r	r
514.96	550	3¼	6¾	12	38¼	r	r
514.96	555	3	r	r	r	43¼	r
514.96	560	2	5⅜	r	47½	49⅝	r
514.96	565	1 7/16	4½	r	r	r	r
514.96	570	1 3/16	3	5⅜	55	61½	r
514.96	575	11/16	r	r	r	58½	r
514.96	580	⅝	r	r	67	67	r
514.96	585	⅜	r	r	r	r	r
514.96	590	¼	r	r	76¼	r	r
514.96	595	3/16	r	r	78½	r	r
514.96	600	r	⅝	1	86	r	r
514.96	605	⅛	r	s	r	r	s
514.96	610	⅛	3/16	r	95	r	r
514.96	615	⅛	r	s	r	r	s
514.96	620	1/16	r	r	r	r	r

Total Call Vol. 13,847 Call Open Int. 40,445
Total Put Vol. 11,691 Put Open Int. 51.873

of a strong upward move in the market before the crisis in the Persian Gulf is resolved. However, this investor is uncertain that the near term negotiations will prove fruitless. The investor is reluctant to completely trade away the upside of the portfolio by writing covered calls for fear of missing the upturn in the market. Given this outlook, the investor decides to take an intermediate position by blending long and short calls. This strategy has the effect of trading away a *well defined portion* of portfolio upside in exchange for option premium.

The investor determines that among optionable indexes, the American Stock Exchange Major Market Index most resembles the portfolio. Exhibit 5-8 displays the Amex MMI options quotes for August 25, 1990 and shows a closing index level of 514.96. The investor decides to explore the next eight weeks as a time horizon for the hedge and therefore focuses on the October contracts. The mechanics of the strategy involve selling call options at one strike level and buying call options at a higher strike level. The exhibit shows the price of an Amex MMI October 515 call is 22.5 or $2,250 and the price of an October 570 call is 3 or $300.

EXHIBIT 5-9

Blended Call Example

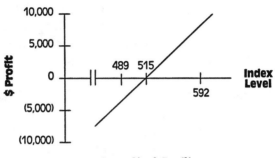

Long Stock Profit

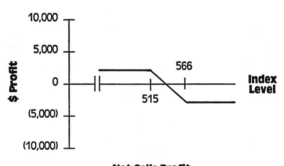

Net Calls Profit

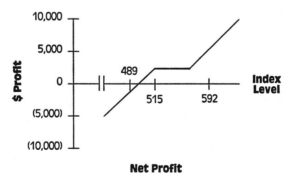

Net Profit

The investor must now decide how many calls will correctly hedge the portfolio. The correct number of 515 calls is 54,250/51,496 = 1 (rounded) and the correct number of 570 calls is 54,250/51,496 = 1 (rounded). Note that in each of the foregoing examples, index levels do not divide evenly into portfolio values making rounding necessary. Some thoughts on rounding are discussed at the end of this section. The investor sells one 515 call and buys one 570 call, receiving net options premiums of 2,250 – 300 = $1950.

Exhibit 5-9 displays the net expiration profit profile that the investor has created through the combination of three strategic building blocks: long stock, short call options and long call options. The investor may expect this net profile to prevail on the third Friday in October 1990 roughly eight weeks in the future. Notice again that the net profile is derived by combining the expiration profiles of the components. The exhibit shows that the investor has traded away only the upside which occurs *between the two strike prices*.

If the market moves below the low strike, the investor receives the expiration profit of the stock portfolio (which is negative) plus net captured option premiums of $1,950. If the market moves between the strikes, the investor receives an approximately level profit roughly equal to the net captured option premiums. If the market moves above the high strike, the investor receives the expiration profit of the portfolio plus net captured option premiums less the difference between the strikes times 100, or {(570-515) x (100)} = $5,500. As before, the net profit at expiration is shown to depend directly on the movement of the index because the example assumes perfect correlation between the index and the underlying portfolio. Basis risk again causes some deviation in expected return. Exhibit 5-10 summarizes the hedge numerically and displays the results of discrete market moves.

On Rounding

In the real world, index levels generally don't divide evenly into portfolio values and investors must round off options positions. Although rounding slightly changes the profits created using options, the necessity for rounding should not discourage investors. Profit tables (like those in the examples) should always be prepared before

EXHIBIT 5-10

Blended Call Example: Calculation of Expiration Profit Profile

Initial Security Statistics

Index Level	514.96
Portfolio Value	$54,250
Strategy	Sell 1 XMI Oct 515 call @ 22 1/2 = $2,250
	Buy 1 XMI Oct 570 call @ 3 = $300

Expiration Profit Profile

Index Change	−5%	0%	5%	10%	15%
Index Level	489.21	514.96	540.71	566.46	592.20
Portfolio Value	$51,538	$54,250	$56,963	$59,675	$62,388
Portfolio Profit	($2,713)	$0	$2,713	$5,425	$8,138
Short Calls Value	$0	$0	($2,571)	($5,146)	($7,720)
Long Calls Value	$0	$0	$0	$0	$2,220
Net Calls Profit	$1,950	$1,950	($621)	($3,196)	($3,550)
Net Profit	($763)	$1,950	$2,092	$2,229	$4,588

initiating an options strategy, and these tables work equally well whether options positions are rounded or not.

SPECULATING

Speculative strategies are aggressive mechanisms for assuming additional but well specified investment risk. They involve index option positions without offsetting positions in stocks. They are generally intended to exploit a particular market outlook by assuming a market exposure that will benefit if an anticipated market move occurs. As emphasized in the earlier chapters, successful speculation will depend largely upon the degree to which the movement of the underlying index corresponds to the actual movement of the market.

Because investor portfolios are typically broadly diversified, hedging strategies most often employ broad-based market indexes. However, speculation does not involve underlying portfolios and this leads to the supposition that broad- and narrow-based indexes are both well suited to speculative strategies. In fact, many people feel that the movements of narrow markets are easier to predict than those of broader ones making the narrow-based indexes uniquely well suited to speculation.

Individual Calls & Puts

Individually, the uses of the four options building blocks as speculative vehicles should be apparent. The long call option can be used when the investor is very bullish on the market, while the long put option can be used when the investor is very bearish. The strike level of these positions should be moderated to reflect the conviction of the investor. Strongly bullish investors should choose higher strikes for a long call, while less certain bulls should choose lower ones. Strongly bearish investors should choose lower strikes for a long put, while less certain bears should choose higher ones. This strike level heuristic for options buyers is designed to maximize return on investment assuming markets move as anticipated.

Similarly, the short call option can be used when the investor is confident the market is not going up, while the short put option can be used when the investor is confident the market is not going down. Again strike levels reflect the conviction of the investor. Investors who feel strongly that the market will not go up should choose lower strikes for a short call, while less confident investors should choose higher strikes. Investors who feel strongly that the market will not go down should choose higher strikes for a short put, while less confident investors should choose lower strikes. The strike level heuristic for options sellers is designed to maximize captured option premiums assuming markets move as anticipated. Remember that writing uncovered options exposes investors to potentially large risks; these positions must be watched very carefully.

Bull Spread

The bull spread is the most popular bullish position among options speculators. The trade is designed to exploit a moderately bullish outlook with downside protection in case expectations are not met.

The mechanics of the trade involve buying call options at one strike level and selling call options at a higher strike level. The bull spread is similar to the blended call hedge except that the strike positions are reversed and no long stock position is held.

Consider an investor who believes that the Persian Gulf crisis will cause energy prices to rise dramatically. Because energy is used at all levels of economic activity, the investor reasons that net price levels in the economy are likely to rise. Economists call this inflation. Historically, people expecting inflation have sought to protect wealth by purchasing precious metals causing the prices of these metals to rise quickly. Therefore, the investor believes that gold and silver prices could rise sharply in the next month. Given this outlook, the investor decides to employ a bull spread on the PHLX Gold & Silver Index.

The investor must now decide which strikes to choose and the appropriate number of options. Exhibit 5-11 displays a reprint of PHLX Gold & Silver options quotes from *Barron's* for the week ending August 27, 1990. *Barron's* reports only those puts and calls that traded over 50 contracts during the prior week, ensuring reasonable liquidity to the investor. The small number of listed quotes evidences the fact that options on this narrow-based index are traded thinly by a small

EXHIBIT 5-11

PHILADELPHIA EXCHANGE

Index Options

GOLD/SILVER INDEX

Expire date Strike price	Sales	Open Int.	Week's High	Low	Net Price Chg.	N.Y. Close
GS Idx Sep110 p	62	34	2½	1¼	2½+ ¾	116.85
GS Idx Sep115 p	56	91	4¼	2⅛	4 + 1⅞	116.85
GS Idx Sep120.	66	131	8⅛	4½	4¾− 3⅝	116.85
GS Idx Sep125.	126	178	6¾	2½	2¾− 3	116.85

EXHIBIT 5-12

Bull Spread Example

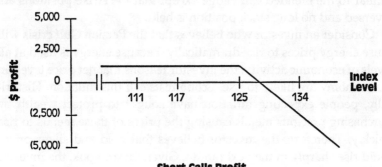

Short Calls Profit

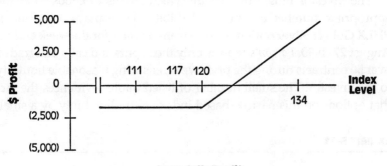

Long Calls Profit

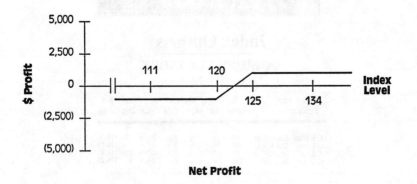

Net Profit

number of players. The investor has no choice of strikes since only two calls are listed. The bull spread requires that the investor buy the lower strike and sell the higher one. The exhibit shows the price of a PHLX GS September 120 call is 4.75 or $475, and the price of 125 call is 2.75 or $275.

The number of options appropriate to the strategy depends upon the investor's resources and appetite for the position. Assume the investor desires exposure roughly equivalent to a $50,000 under-lying value. The correct number of options for the strategy is 50,000/11,685 = 4 (rounded). The investor buys four of the low strike options and sells four of the high strike options at net cost of $800.

Exhibit 5-12 displays the net expiration profit profile which the investor has created through combination of two strategic building blocks: long and short call options. The investor may expect this net profile to prevail on the third Friday in September 1990 roughly four weeks in the future. Notice again that the net profile is derived by combining the expiration profiles of the two component building blocks. The exhibit shows that the bull spread strategy limits both upside and downside while retaining a clearly bullish preference. The investor has achieved an exposure which is sensitive only to market movement *between the two strike prices.*

If the market remains below or moves to the low strike, both options positions expire worthless, and the investor receives the net of the premiums, or an $800 loss. As the market moves between the two strikes, the investor receives the action of the market. If the market moves to or above the high strike, the investor receives the maximum gain of $1200. Exhibit 5-13 summarizes the hedge numerically and displays the results of discrete market moves.

Bear Spread

The bear spread is the most popular bearish position among op-tions speculators. The trade is designed to exploit a moderately bear-ish outlook with upside protection in case expectations are not met. The mechanics of the trade involve selling put options at one strike level and buying put options at a higher strike level. The bear spread is exactly the reverse of the bull spread trade.

EXHIBIT 5-13

Bull Spread Example: Calculation of Expiration Profit Profile

Initial Security Statistics

Index Level	116.85
Exposure	$50,000
Strategy	Sell 4 XAU Sep 125 calls @ 2 3/4 = $1,100
	Buy 4 XAU Sep 120 calls @ 4 3/4 = $1,900

Expiration Profit Profile

Index Change	–5%	0%	5%	10%	15%
Index Level	111.01	116.85	122.69	128.54	134.38
Short Calls Value	$0	$0	$0	($1,414)	($3,751)
Short Calls Profit	$1,100	$1,100	$1,100	($314)	($2,651)
Long Calls Value	$0	$0	$1,077	$3,414	$5,751
Long Calls Profit	($1,900)	($1,900)	($823)	$1,514	$3,851
Net Profit	($800)	($800)	$277	$1,200	$1,200

Consider an investor who believes that the Persian Gulf crisis has already caused energy prices to rise too much. The investor is convinced that the markets have over-reacted to the Iraqi invasion, and that energy prices are likely to fall when participants correctly assess the situation. Therefore, the investor feels strongly that energy prices could fall sharply in the next month. Given this outlook, the investor decides to employ a bear spread on the AMEX Oil Index.

The investor must now decide which strikes to choose and the appropriate number of options. Exhibit 5-14 displays a reprint of AMEX Oil options quotes from *Barron's* for the week ending August 24, 1990. *Barron's* reports only those puts and calls that traded over 50 contracts during the prior week, ensuring reasonable liquidity to the investor. The small number of listed quotes evidences the fact that options on this narrow-based index are traded thinly by a small number of players. The investor has no choice of strikes since only two puts are listed. The bear spread requires that the investor sell the lower strike and buy the higher one. The exhibit shows the price of an

EXHIBIT 5-14

AMERICAN EXCHANGE

Index Options

OIL INDEX

Expire date Strike price		Sales	Open Int.	Week's High	Low	Price	Net Chg.	N.Y. Close
Oil Idx	Sep240 p	75	40	3½	½	2¾	+ ¾	256.49
Oil Idx	Sep265 p	59	111	8⅞	5⅛	8⅞	+ 2⅞	256.49
Oil Idx	Sep270.	55	29	9⅛	2½	2½	− 5¼	256.49
Oil Idx	Sep285.	276	182	2⅜	¾	¾	− 1⅜	256.49
Oil Idx	Oct280.	100	100	6⅝	6⅝	6⅝	......	256.49

AMEX September 240 put is 2.75 or $275, and the price of 265 put is 8.875 or $887.50.

As before, the number of options appropriate to the strategy depends upon the investor's resources and appetite for the position. Assume the investor desires exposure roughly equivalent to a $50,000 underlying value. The correct number of options for the strategy is 50,000/25,649 = 2 (rounded). The investor sells two of the low strike options and buys two of the high strike options at net cost of $1,225.

Exhibit 5-15 displays the net expiration profit profile that the investor has created through combination of two strategic building blocks: long and short put options. The investor may expect this net profile to prevail on the third Friday in September 1990 roughly four weeks in the future. Notice again that the net profile is derived by combining the expiration profiles of the two component building blocks. The exhibit shows that the bear spread strategy limits both upside and downside while retaining a clearly bearish preference. As with the bull spread, the bear spread investor achieves an exposure that is sensitive only to market movement *between the two strike prices.*

If the market moves to or above the high strike, both options

EXHIBIT 5-15

Bear Spread Example

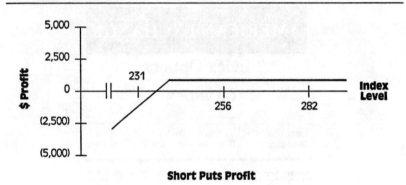

Short Puts Profit

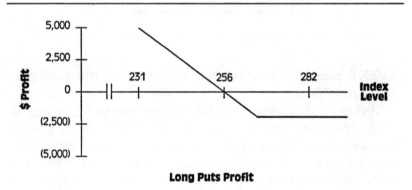

Long Puts Profit

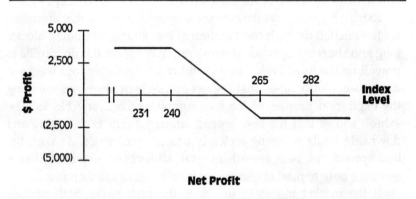

Net Profit

EXHIBIT 5-16

Bear Spread Example: Calculation of Expiration Profit Profile

Initial Security Statistics

Index Level	256.49
Exposure	$50,000
Strategy	Sell 2 XOI Sep 240 puts @ 2 3/4 = $ 550
	Buy 2 XOI Sep 265 puts @ 8 7/8 = $1,775

Expiration Profit Profile

Index Change	−10%	−5%	0%	5%	10%
Index Level	230.84	243.67	256.49	269.31	282.14
Short Puts Value	($1,832)	$0	$0	$0	$0
Short Puts Profit	($1,282)	$550	$550	$550	$550
Long Puts Value	$6,832	$4,267	$1,702	$0	$0
Long Puts Profit	$5,057	$2,492	($73)	($1,775)	($1,775)
Net Profit	$3,775	$3,042	$477	($1,225)	($1,225)

positions expire worthless, and the investor receives the net of the premiums, or a $1225 loss. As the market moves between the two strikes, the investor receives the short action of the market. If the market moves to or below the low strike, the investor receives the maximum gain of $3,775. Exhibit 5-16 summarizes the hedge numerically and displays the results of discrete market moves.

Long Straddle

The long straddle is a classic high volatility bet among options speculators. The trade is designed to exploit an expectation that the market will experience near term volatility without regard for direction. The mechanics of the trade involve buying call and put options at the same strike level. Although expensive to implement, the long straddle produces unlimited profit potential with limited downside.

Consider an investor who is unsure about the outcome of the Persian Gulf crisis, but feels confident that the crisis will continue to produce high market volatility. Given this outlook, the investor decides to employ a long straddle on the S&P 100 Index.

EXHIBIT 5-17

CHICAGO BOARD

Index Options

S&P 100 INDEX OEX

Expire date Strike price		Sales	Open Int.	Week's High	Low	Price	Net Chg.	N.Y. Close
SP100	Sep285..	1440	232	24	14½	18¼	......	296.68
SP100	Sep285 p	36972	21365	10	3	6½	......	296.68
SP100	Sep290..	14154	7813	22¼	8½	14¾	......	296.68
SP100	Sep290 p	28046	20016	11⅝	3⅞	7¾	......	296.68
SP100	Sep295..	8499	5006	17¾	7¾	11⅝	......	296.68
SP100	Sep295 p	24116	12828	13½	4⅞	9½	......	296.68
SP100	Sep300..	33563	17334	19¼	5¾	8½	−10	296.68
SP100	Sep300 p	52374	33161	16¼	4⅜	11⅝	+ 5¾	296.68
SP100	Sep305..	10868	17011	15½	3¾	5⅝	− 9⅞	296.68
SP100	Sep305 p	31768	27010	19¼	5½	13¼	+ 6⅛	296.68
SP100	Sep310..	21517	28873	11¾	2½	3¾	− 7	296.68
SP100	Sep310 p	50597	39328	22⅜	6⅞	17	+ 8⅜	296.68
SP100	Sep315..	10252	27085	8½	1 7-16	2½	− 5⅜	296.68
SP100	Sep315 p	24977	25586	27	8¾	20½	+ 9¾	296.68
SP100	Sep320	20767	27900	5⅝	¾	1 11-16	−3 5-16	296.68
SP100	Sep320 p	28763	25390	31½	10¾	25	+12	296.68
SP100	Sep325..	28106	25448	3¾	7-16	⅞	− 2½	296.68
SP100	Sep325 p	18278	17085	36	14	29½	+13⅜	296.68
SP100	Sep330	28444	23364	2 3-16	5-16	½	−1 9-16	296.68
SP100	Sep330 p	13109	18028	41	17⅝	35	+15¼	296.68
SP100	Sep335..	27411	21879	1¼	3-16	5-16	−15-16	296.68
SP100	Sep335 p	8711	10916	46½	22	39⅜	+14⅝	296.68
SP100	Sep340..	22478	25977	¾	⅛	¼	− ½	296.68
SP100	Sep340 p	10884	12734	50⅛	26½	44¼	+14¾	296.68
SP100	Sep345..	14403	19252	½	⅛	3-16	− ¼	296.68
SP100	Sep345 p	4668	3564	54	31	50	+15½	296.68
SP100	Sep350...	7609	17718	5-16	1-16	⅛	−3-16	296.68
SP100	Sep350 p	1349	2089	60¼	36¼	54	+14⅜	296.68
SP100	Sep355..	5376	9167	3-16	1-16	1-16	− ⅛	296.68
SP100	Sep360...	3637	12300	⅛	1-16	1-16	−1-16	296.68
SP100	Sep365..	395	10737	1-16	1-16	1-16	......	296.68
SP100	Oct280 p	1599	.....	11¼	8¾	9½	......	296.68
SP100	Oct285..	154	150	23	21¼	21½	......	296.68
SP100	Oct285 p	7660	3401	14	5⅛	10⅜	......	296.68
SP100	Oct290..	538	54	19½	16¼	16⅜	......	296.68
SP100	Oct290 p	9886	6122	15¾	6⅜	12	......	296.68
SP100	Oct295..	1669	468	16¾	13	15¼	......	296.68
SP100	Oct295 p	3659	2108	17	8⅛	13⅜	......	296.68
SP100	Oct300..	2480	2032	19¼	10	13	−14⅜	296.68
SP100	Oct300 p	14492	7672	19¼	7	15½	+ 7⅝	296.68
SP100	Oct305..	2733	1766	15¼	8¼	10	......	296.68
SP100	Oct305 p	5638	3014	22	8¼	18¼	+ 8⅞	296.68
SP100	Oct310..	1730	1247	15⅜	6	8	− 6⅞	296.68
SP100	Oct310 p	6753	4935	25	9¾	20	+ 9	296.68
SP100	Oct315..	4870	3020	12¼	4⅜	5⅜	− 6⅜	296.68
SP100	Oct315 p	3917	2201	28½	11½	24	+11	296.68
SP100	Oct320..	7348	8990	9½	3	4⅜	− 5⅛	296.68
SP100	Oct320 p	10431	11951	34	13¾	27	+12¼	296.68
SP100	Oct325	4147	3337	7	2	2 11-16	−3 13-16	296.68
SP100	Oct325 p	1866	4264	36	16	31	+13¾	296.68
SP100	Oct330..	6542	4383	5	1 7-16	2	− 3	296.68
SP100	Oct330 p	3619	3253	40½	19½	35½	+14⅝	296.68
SP100	Oct335..	3263	3735	3⅜	15-16	1⅜	− 2	296.68
SP100	Oct335 p	1536	2739	46	24	40¾	+14¾	296.68
SP100	Oct340..	5405	5643	2½	11-16	⅞	− 1⅜	296.68
SP100	Oct340 p	2640	3023	51	26⅝	48	+21	296.68
SP100	Oct345	8332	4580	1¾	7-16	½	−1 1-16	296.68
SP100	Oct345 p	4222	2352	56	31	51½	+17	296.68
SP100	Oct350..	4584	2746	1	⅜	⅜	− ½	296.68
SP100	Oct350 p	152	605	59½	36½	56¼	+17⅜	296.68
SP100	Oct355..	2792	9855	⅝	¼	5-16	− ¼	296.68
SP100	Oct360...	663	3944	⅜	3-16	3-16	−3-16	296.68
SP100	Oct365..	733	4738	5-16	⅛	⅛	− ⅛	296.68
SP100	Nov285 p	827	580	15¾	8⅛	13¼	......	296.68
SP100	Nov290..	50	80	19½	16½	19½	......	296.68
SP100	Nov290 p	832	655	17¾	9	15	......	296.68
SP100	Nov300..	450	324	21	13	16	− 6	296.68
SP100	Nov300 p	3148	2118	22	9¼	18	+ 8⅜	296.68
SP100	Nov305 p	294	179	25	12¼	21¾	......	296.68
SP100	Nov310..	844	1021	18	8	9¾	− 6¼	296.68
SP100	Nov310 p	944	1384	28	12¼	25¼	+11½	296.68
SP100	Nov315..	381	347	11⅜	7	8¼	......	296.68
SP100	Nov315 p	153	1610	31½	17	28½	......	296.68
SP100	Nov320..	650	1829	9¼	5¼	6	− 5	296.68
SP100	Nov320 p	1389	1761	35	16½	31	+14½	296.68
SP100	Nov325 p	52	36	37	25	33¾	......	296.68
SP100	Nov330..	231	1041	7	2¾	3	− 4	296.68
SP100	Nov330 p	2329	1813	43	21	40	+16½	296.68
SP100	Nov335..	315	86	4¼	1¾	1⅞	......	296.68
SP100	Nov340..	2361	1463	3¾	1¼	1½	− 2¼	296.68
SP100	Nov340 p	1196	1473	50	28½	45	+15¾	296.68
SP100	Nov345..	533	410	1¾	1	1¼	......	296.68
SP100	Nov350.	1893	2056	2⅛	⅝	11-16	−1 5-16	296.68
SP100	Nov360..	804	1360	1	½	½	− ⅜	296.68
SP100	Dec290..	326	326	21	20	20¼	......	296.68
SP100	Dec290 p	632	1783	18½	11	18	......	296.68
SP100	Dec310..	488	414	16	11⅞	11⅞	......	296.68

The investor must now decide which strikes to choose and the appropriate number of options. Exhibit 5-17 displays a reprint of S&P 100 options quotes from *Barron's* for the week ending August 25, 1990. *Barron's* reports only those puts and calls that traded over 50 contracts during the prior week, ensuring reasonable liquidity to the investor. The large number of listed quotes evidences the fact that options on this broad-based index are traded widely by a large number of players. In fact, the S&P 100 index option is the most heavily traded of all stock index options. The investor has many choices of strikes, and chooses 295 because it is closest to the previous day's close. The exhibit shows the price of an S&P 100 September 295 call is 11.625 or $1,162.50, and the price of a 295 put is 9.5 or $950.

As before, the number of options appropriate to the strategy depends upon the investor's resources and appetite for the position. Assume the investor desires exposure roughly equivalent to a $60,000 underlying value. The correct number of options for the strategy is 60,000/29,668 = 2 (rounded). The investor buys two of each option at net cost of $4,225.

Exhibit 5-18 displays the net expiration profit profile which the investor has created through combination of two strategic building blocks: long call and put options. The investor may expect this net profile to prevail on the third Friday in September 1990 roughly four weeks in the future. Notice again that the net profile is derived by combining the expiration profiles of the two component building blocks. The exhibit shows that the long straddle generates profits regardless of which direction the market moves. However, the long straddle investor achieves profit only when the market makes a large move. Exhibit 5-19 summarizes the hedge numerically and displays the results of discrete market moves.

Short Straddle

The short straddle is a classic market stagnation bet among options speculators. The trade is designed to exploit an expectation that the market will experience near term stagnation. The mechanics of the trade involve selling call and put options at the same strike level. Although the short straddle produces unlimited loss potential, it generates significant income in the form of captured option premiums.

Consider an investor who is unsure about the outcome of the Persian Gulf crisis, but feels confident that the crisis will immobilize the markets until resolved. Given this outlook, the investor decides to employ a short straddle on the S&P 100 Index.

The investor must now decide which strikes to choose and the appropriate number of options. Returning to Exhibit 5-17, the investor decides to use the same options which were used to illustrate the long straddle in the prior example. The exhibit shows the price of an S&P 100 September 295 call is 11.625 or $1,162.50, and the price of a 295 put is 9.5 or $950.

As before, the number of options appropriate to the strategy de-

EXHIBIT 5-18

Long Straddle Example

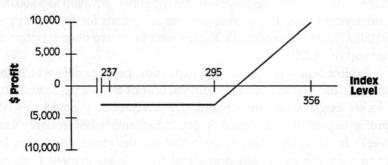

Long Calls Profit

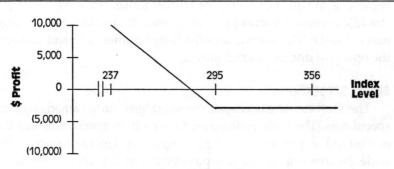

Long Puts Profit

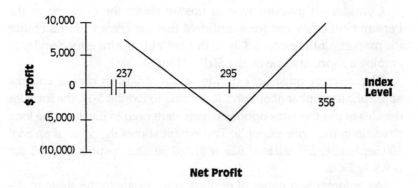

Net Profit

EXHIBIT 5-19

Long Straddle Example: Calculation of Expiration Profit Profile

Initial Security Statistics

Index Level	296.68
Exposure	$60,000
Strategy	Buy 2 OEX Sep 295 calls @ 11 5/8 = $2,325
	Buy 2 OEX Sep 295 puts @ 9 1/2 = $1,900

Expiration Profit Profile

Index Change	-20%	-10%	0%	10%	20%
Index Level	237.34	267.01	296.68	326.35	356.02
Long Calls Value	$0	$0	$336	$6,270	$12,203
Long Calls Profit	($2,325)	($2,325)	($1,989)	$3,945	$9,878
Long Puts Value	$11,531	$5,598	$0	$0	$0
Long Puts Profit	$9,631	$3,698	($1,900)	($1,900)	($1,900)
Net Profit	$7,306	$1,373	($3,889)	$2,045	$7,978

pends upon the investor's resources and appetite for the position. Assume the investor desires exposure roughly equivalent to a $60,000 underlying value. The correct number of options for the strategy is 60,000/29,668 = 2 (rounded). The investor sells two of each option at net captured option premium of $4,225.

Exhibit 5-20 displays the net expiration profit profile that the investor has created through combination of two strategic building blocks: short call and put options. The investor may expect this net profile to prevail on the third Friday in September 1990 roughly four weeks in the future. Notice, yet again, that the net profile is derived by combining the expiration profiles of the two component building blocks. The exhibit shows that the short straddle generates losses only when the market moves. As long as the markets are stagnant, the investor captures option premiums without liability. Exhibit 5-21 summarizes the hedge numerically and displays the results of discrete market moves.

EXHIBIT 5-20

Short Straddle Example

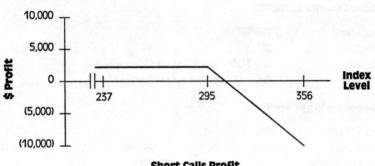

Short Calls Profit

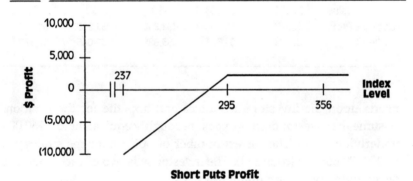

Short Puts Profit

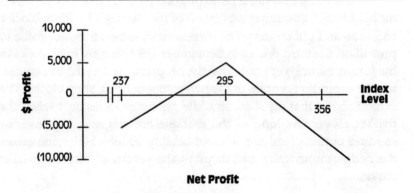

Net Profit

EXHIBIT 5-21

Short Straddle Example: Calculation of Expiration Profit Profile

Initial Security Statistics

Index Level	296.68
Exposure	$60,000
Strategy	Sell 2 OEX Sep 295 calls @ 11 5/8 = $2,325
	Sell 2 OEX Sep 295 puts @ 9 1/2 = $1,900

Expiration Profit Profile

Index Change	−20%	−10%	0%	10%	20%
Index Level	237.34	267.01	296.68	326.35	356.02
Short Calls Value	$0	$0	($336)	($6,270)	($12,203)
Short Calls Profit	$2,325	$2,325	$1,989	($3,945)	($9,878)
Short Puts Value	($11,531)	($5,598)	$0	$0	$0
Short Puts Profit	($9,631)	($3,698)	$1,900	$1,900	$1,900
Net Profit	($7,306)	($1,373)	$3,889	($2,045)	($7,978)

LOOKING AHEAD

This concludes the examination of classic options strategies. Based on the information presented in all preceding chapters, readers should now have a strong foundation upon which personal options strategies can be built. However, up to this point only short term options have been discussed. Chapter 6 will cover longer term index options and strategies.

LOOKING AHEAD

6

Long Term
Index Options

Chapter 5 combined concepts developed earlier in the book to explore classic option strategies. These strategies demonstrated that a variety of payoff profiles can be created using securities combinations to suit various investment outlooks and risk tolerances. One limitation of the foregoing, however, was the relatively short time horizons explored. Traditionally, listed stock index options have demanded short planning horizons because available expiration dates were relatively near term. Investors seeking longer term exposures were forced to utilize successive short dated options to achieve their goals.

In late 1987 the CBOE introduced the SPL index option, a long term version of the standardized contract available for the S&P 500 stock index. The SPL has expirations available for up to two years. Unfortunately, the timing of this product introduction coincided with the stock market crash of October 19, 1987. This ill-fated coincidence overshadowed the SPL such that it has never achieved the market participation anticipated for it by CBOE. Hence, liquidity for the SPL has typically been poor. In early 1991, CBOE introduced a new series of long term options to the market under the acronym LEAPS (Long Term Equity Anticipation Product). About the same time AMEX also introduced a long term option, the LT-20.

The introduction of these instruments was accompanied by intensive media campaigns designed to build market awareness and participation quickly. The ultimate success of the options is as yet unclear. However, long term index options are significant because they enable investors to employ 2 to 3 year options strategies with the same ease, convenience (and hopefully liquidity) previously available only for much shorter time horizons. This chapter will not explore the SPL but will focus on key features of the newer long term options and explore their use for two long term index option strategies.

UNDERLYING INDEXES

The indexes which underlie these long term options are calculated as fractions of pre-existing optionable indexes. The underlying index for the AMEX LT-20 is calculated as 1/20th of the AMEX Major Market Index. The underlying index for the CBOE OEX-Leaps is calculated as 1/10th of the S&P 100 Index, and the underlying index for the CBOE SPX-Leaps is calculated as 1/10th of the S&P 500 Index. Thus, it is clear that these new options are simply longer term versions of previously discussed stock index options. The index construction and historical correlations presented in Chapters 2 and 3 would apply equally well in the context of the shorter or longer dated options.

EXPIRATION SCHEDULES

In January of 1991, two expiration series were available for Leaps contracts and the LT-20 contract. These series expire in December 1992 and 1993. Series with 36 months to expiration are intended to be introduced each December in the future. All contracts follow the established index option convention of expiration on the Saturday following the third Friday of the expiration month.

LIQUIDITY

Despite their newness, liquidity in these contracts has already achieved levels that compare favorably to other broad-based index options. For example, on January 29 1991, open interests in the LT-20s were 27,708 calls and 61,171 puts, compared to 49,166 calls and 38,351 puts on the traditional Major Market Index. On the same day, open interests in the NYSE Composite Index were only 4,744 calls and 2,292 puts; open interests in the Financial News Composite Index were only 2,769 calls and 1,147 puts; open interests in the S&P 500 Leaps were 11,000 calls and 17,235 puts.

PRICE LEVELS

These indexes underlying long term options are computed as fractions of pre-existing indexes. Therefore, price levels of the indexes underlying long term options are fractions of pre-existing index price levels. As discussed in Chapter 2, the price level of an underlying index is an important consideration that can justifiably influence the index selection decision. This is because index price levels impact option contract values. More contracts on a lower priced index must be purchased to obtain dollar exposure equal to that obtained with fewer contracts on a higher priced index. For example, it would take twenty LT-20 contracts to obtain dollar exposure equal to that obtained with one XMI contract. Because they correspond to relatively small dollar exposures, the LT-20 and Leaps contracts are particularly well suited to investors seeking to hedge or speculate on smaller positions.

LONG-TERM INDEX OPTION STRATEGIES

Long-term index options can be used to implement any of the strategies discussed in Chapter 5. However, the long term nature of these options suits them particularly to certain strategies not previously discussed. Two of these strategies follow.

Portfolio Substitution

Consider an investor in January 1991 with $26,000 to invest in the stock market. The investor believes that the next two years could be very good for the stock market, but remains uncomfortable with

EXHIBIT 6-1

INDEX TRADING

Wednesday, January 30, 1991
OPTIONS

Chicago Board

Strike	LEAPS-S&P 100 INDEX				
	Calls—Last		Puts—Last		
Price	Dec92	Dec 93	Dec 92	Dec 93	
27½	....	7¾	....	1 13/16	....	....
30	5¼	....	....	2 7/16	....	....
32½	4	....	....	3½	....	....

Total call volume 110 Total call open int. 4,710
Total put volume 497 Total put open int. 20,569
The index: High 32.31; Low 31.74; Close 32.31, +0.57

unprotected exposure to equities. This investor could purchase a well diversified stock portfolio in combination with two year protective puts. However, a less costly strategy which creates a similar profit profile is the purchase of two-year index calls in combination with two year US Treasury securities.

Assume the investor is interested in tracking the performance of the S&P 100. Exhibit 6-1 displays the OEX-Leaps options quotes for January 30, 1991 as published in the *Wall Street Journal*. The exhibit shows a closing index level of 32.31. (This implies that the S&P 100 index closed at 323.1.) The investor has a two year outlook and therefore chooses the 1992 contract; and is a fairly confident bull and therefore chooses the higher of the two available strikes. The exhibit shows that the price of an OEX-Leaps December 1992 32.5 call is 4 or $400.

The investor must now determine how many calls should be purchased. Given $26,000 to invest, the investor desires exposure roughly equivalent to a $26,000 underlying value. That is, the investor wants to obtain exposure that approximates that obtained if the entire $26,000 were invested in the stocks that comprise the index. The correct number of options for the strategy is 26,000/3231 = 8 (rounded). The investor buys the eight options for a cost of $3200 and uses the remainder of the available funds to purchase two year Treasury notes yielding 7.0%.

Exhibit 6-2 displays the net expiration profit profile that the investor has created through combination of two strategic building blocks: long call options and US Treasury notes. The investor may expect this net profile to prevail on the third Friday in December 1992 roughly two years hence. As always, the net profile is derived by combining the expiration profiles of the two component elements of the strategy. The exhibit shows that the portfolio substitution strategy has retained unlimited market upside while limiting market downside. This profile is similar to that produced by purchasing long call options alone, however in this case the interest earned on the Treasury notes cushions the downside.

Exhibit 6-3 summarizes the example numerically and compares the strategy to the alternative investment of all $26,000 in the stocks that make up the index. The strategy performs similarly to the long stock alternative in a rising market, however it protects the investor from large potential losses in a falling market. Remember, that for simplicity of presentation, the example ignores transactions costs.

Market Fence

Consider an investor in January 1991 with a portfolio that resembles the Dow worth $26,000. Concerned about the direction of the market over the next two years, the investor wishes to protect the portfolio against downside risk but does not wish to pay for protective puts. The investor can achieve this objective by utilizing a market fence. Using a fence, the investor buys downside protection for the portfolio (long, an out-of-the-money put), and finances it by selling the market upside of the portfolio (short, an out-of-the-money call).

After careful analysis of the portfolio relative to available long term optionable indexes, the investor decides the portfolio is best matched to the AMEX Major Market. Exhibit 6-4 displays the LT-20 options quotes for January 29, 1991 as published in the *Wall Street*

EXHIBIT 6-2

Portfolio Substitution Example

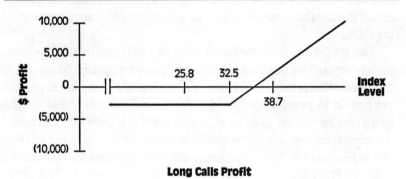

Long Calls Profit

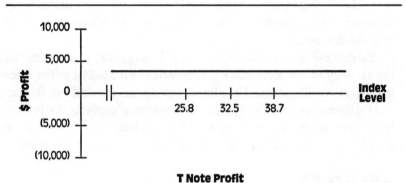

T Note Profit

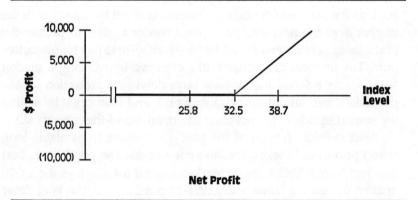

Net Profit

EXHIBIT 6-3

Portfolio Substitution Example: Calculation of Expiration Profit Profile

Initial Security Statistics

Index Level	32.31
Exposure	$26,000
Strategy	Buy 8 OEX-Leaps Dec '92 32.5 calls @ 4 = $3,200
	Buy $22,800 2yr US Treasury Notes yielding 7%

Expiration Profit Profile

Index Change	−20%	−10%	0%	10%	20%
Index Level	25.85	29.08	32.31	35.54	38.77
Long Calls Value	$0	$0	$0	$2,433	$5,018
Long Calls Profit	($3,200)	($3,200)	($3,200)	($767)	$1,818
T-Notes Profit	$3,192	$3,192	$3,192	$3,192	$3,192
Net Profit	($8)	($8)	($8)	$2,425	$5,010
Stock Only Profit	($5,200)	($2,600)	$0	$2,600	$5,200

EXHIBIT 6-4

INDEX TRADING

Wednesday, January 30, 1991

OPTIONS

American Exchange

LT-20 INDEX

Strike	Calls—Last			Puts—Last		
Price	Dec 92	Dec 93		Dec 92	Dec 93	
25	5¼	5¾	....	1 5/16	1¾	....
27½	....	....	....	2⅛	....	....
30	2⅝	....	....	3⅛	....	....

Total call volume 1,883   Total call open int. 27,708
Total put volume 2,775   Total put open int. 61,171
The index: High 28.36; Low 27.88; Close 28.36, +0.47

EXHIBIT 6-5

Market Fence Example

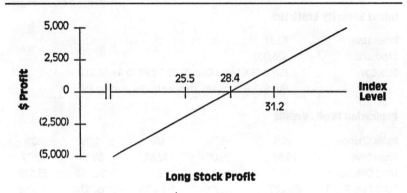

Long Stock Profit

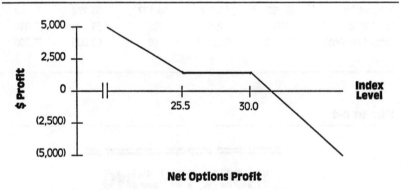

Net Options Profit

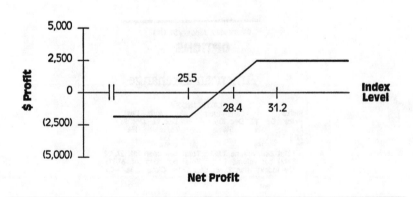

Net Profit

EXHIBIT 6-6

Market Fence Example: Calculation of Expiration Profit Profile

Initial Security Statistics

Index Level	28.36
Portfolio Value	$26,000
Strategy	Sell 9 LT-20 Dec '92 30 calls @ 2.625 = $2,362.50
	Buy 9 LT-20 Dec '92 25 puts @ 1.3125 = $1,181.25

Expiration Profit Profile

Index Change	−20%	−10%	0%	10%	20%
Index Level	22.69	25.52	28.36	31.20	34.03
Portfolio Value	$20,800	$23,400	$26,000	$28,600	$31,200
Portfolio Profit	($5,200)	($2,600)	$0	$2,600	$5,200
Short Calls Value	$0	$0	$0	($1,076)	($3,629)
Long Puts Value	$2,081	$0	$0	$0	$0
Net Options Profit	$3,262	$1,181	$1,181	$105	($2,448)
Net Profit	($1,938)	($1,419)	$1,181	$2,705	$2,752

Journal. The exhibit shows a closing index level of 28.36. (This implies that the Major Market index closed at 567.2.) The investor has a two year outlook and therefore chooses the 1992 contract. The exhibit shows the price of an LT-20 December 1992 30 call is 2.625 or $262.50, and the price of a December 1992 25 put is 1.3125 or $131.25.

The investor must now determine how many options should be purchased. The correct number of options for the strategy is 26,000/ 2836 = 9 (rounded). The investor buys the nine put options and sells nine call options for a net captured option premium of of $1,181.25.

Exhibit 6-5 displays the net expiration profit profile that the investor has created through combination of three strategic building blocks: long stock, long put options, and short call options. The investor may expect this net profile to prevail on the third Friday in December 1992 roughly two years hence. As always, the net profile is derived by combining the expiration profiles of the two component elements of the strategy. The exhibit shows that the strategy has "fenced" the portfolio into a narrow range of possible expiration values. The portfolio is protected against index movement below the low strike, however the investor has achieved this protection at no cost by trading upside potential above the high strike. Exhibit 6-6 summarizes the example numerically and displays the results of discrete market moves.

LOOKING AHEAD

This concludes the examination of long term listed options. Contract specifications for the LT-20 and Leaps options can be found in Appendix C. Chapter 7 will discuss option valuation as a prerequisite to the option replication strategy presented in Chapter 8.

7

Index Option Valuation

Chapters 5 and 6 demonstrated graphical and numerical payoff profiles for index options at expiration. The discussion showed that at expiration, only two factors impinge upon the value of an option: the strike price and the price of the underlying index. Implicit in this presentation was the appropriate precept that option strategies are typically employed with a view to the outcome of the strategy at the expiration date. However, all options investors must acquire positions prior to expiration and certain options investors will liquidate their positions prior to expiration. Therefore, valuation during the option's life is an important skill for any option investor. This chapter will explore the valuation of index options prior to expiration.

TIME VALUE PREMIUM

At expiration, in-the-money option values are computed as the difference between the strike and underlying prices times the contract multiplier. Out-of-the-money options have zero value at expiration, i.e., they expire worthless. The option value computed in this way is called intrinsic value. Although intrinsic value is a good measure of value at expiration, options are generally worth more than intrinsic value prior to expiration. This additional value is called time value premium. (This should not be confused with the amount paid for an option, called the option premium.) Thus, prior to expiration, total option value is equal to intrinsic value plus time value premium.

Certain factors which determine time value premiums have been identified and studied thoroughly. Five such factors can be measured and quantified. The most significant is the relationship between the strike and underlying price. The other factors are time until expiration, index volatility, the prevailing level of interest rates, and index dividends.

Relationship Between Strike & Underlying Prices

Exhibit 7-1 displays the effect of the first factor, the relationship between the strike and underlying prices. The exhibit plots the option price as a function of underlying price, illustrating both intrinsic value (price at expiration) and total value (price prior to expiration). The

EXHIBIT 7-1

Time Value Premium

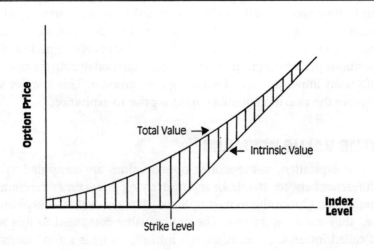

shaded area is the time value premium which is the value of the option in excess of intrinsic value. As the exhibit shows, options well out-of-the-money or options well in-the-money carry very small premiums. The greatest premium occurs when the strike and underlying prices are equal.

Time Until Expiration

Exhibit 7-2 displays the effect of the second factor, the time until expiration. The exhibit repeats the previous format, but represents total value at several remaining times to expiration. As the exhibit shows, options with long remaining times to expiration generally have greater time value premiums than equivalent options with shorter remaining times. This occurs because the longer dated option allows more opportunity for the market to move, and this move could be favorable to the option holder. As time passes, the time value premium gradually decays, disappearing at expiration when only intrinsic value remains.

EXHIBIT 7-2

Time Value Premium at Various Times Until Expiration

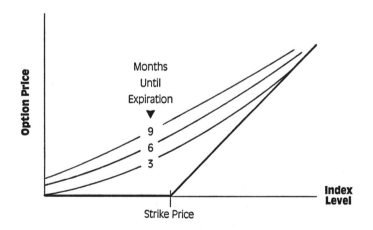

95

EXHIBIT 7-3

Decay of Time Value Premium

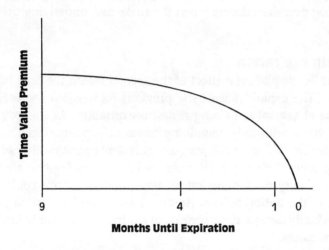

Exhibit 7-3 displays the erosion of time value premium in a different perspective. This exhibit plots the time value premium as a function of time remaining to expiration. As the exhibit shows, time value premium decay is not linear as one might expect. For a long life option, the time value declines rather slowly when the option is new. As the option ages, there is an acceleration in the rate at which the time value decays.

Index Volatility

The third factor which contributes to time value premiums is volatility of the underlying index. Options on volatile underlying indexes generally have greater time value premiums than equivalent options on stable underlying indexes. This occurs because volatile indexes are more likely to make a large move, and this move could be favorable to the option holder. The value associated with volatility is captured in the time value shown in Exhibit 7-1.

Prevailing Interest Rates

The fourth factor which contributes to time value premiums is the interest rate available on a risk free asset, such as a 90-day US Treasury bill. When the risk free rate is high, time value premiums are greater than when it is low. This factor is related to the use of the risk free asset in a strategy to replicate the option. If the option is not valued correctly it can be replicated more cheaply or more expensively than it can be bought, creating opportunity for arbitrage profits. Therefore, the prevailing level of interest rates affects option valuation. The value associated with the risk free rate is also captured in the time value shown in Exhibit 7-1.

Dividends

The fifth factor which contributes to time value premiums is the aggregate dividend paid on the stocks in the underlying index. Options on high dividend indexes generally have smaller time value premiums than equivalent options on indexes paying low aggregate dividends. This occurs because stockholders are entitled to dividends while option holders are not. Thus, when high dividends are paid the stock becomes increasingly valuable relative to the option. The value associated with the dividend is also captured in the time value shown in Exhibit 7-1.

BLACK-SCHOLES MODEL

The factors discussed above are the only readily quantifiable contributors to option value in excess of intrinsic value—the time value premium. In the real world, however, non-quantifiable factors such as investor psychology also influence time value premium. By comparing the theoretical price (computed using quantifiable factors) against the market price, investors can gain insight into the current market psychology and make judgements about the fairness of observed option price levels.

Several mathematical formulas have have been derived to provide the theoretical price at which an option should trade given the quantifiable factors which affect option pricing. These formulas are elaborate and are best left to sophisticated computer software. However, some insight into the process can be given here without introducing unduly complex mathematics.

The best known model and probably the one which is most widespread is that of Black and Scholes introduced in 1973. The general equation for the model is shown in Exhibit 7-4. The Black-Scholes model is a milestone in the world of finance and it has been widely accepted and used. Although elegant, it does have some basic shortcomings which affect its accuracy. Most notably, the model does not incorporate dividends into the computation of option price. Fortunately, a simple adjustment can incorporate dividends into the solution with a high degree of accuracy.

Estimating Volatility

As discussed above, there are five quantifiable factors that affect the value of an option. With the exception of dividends, these factors are the inputs for the Black-Scholes formula. Most of these inputs are easy to get. The index level is published in the newspaper and the desired strike level is determined by the investor. The time horizon for the strategy is also investor determined and the risk free rate of interest can be set at some realistic level such as the current yield of the investor's money market fund or the 90-day T-bill.

The tricky input, and one which will make a big difference in the computation, is the volatility of the underlying index. Volatility is a measure of an index's propensity to change over a period of time. It is generally computed from historical data—weekly or daily prices going back as much as five years. More precisely, volatility is a statistical computation of the annualized standard deviation of index price changes.

Unfortunately, the volatility of indexes like the S&P 500 have been historically unstable. Between 1978 and 1987, the S&P 500 had a mean volatility (standard deviation) of about 15%; however, it reached a high of 24% in 1982 and a low of 9% in 1984. For option strategies, investors must attempt to estimate what the volatility of the underlying index will be over the life of the strategy. The inherent instability

EXHIBIT 7-4

Black-Scholes Model

$$Q_c = SN(d_1) - EN(d_2)e^{-rt}$$

$$d_1 = \frac{\ln \frac{S}{E} + (r + \frac{1}{2}s^2)t}{s\sqrt{t}}$$

$$d_2 = \frac{\ln \frac{S}{E} + (r - \frac{1}{2}s^2)t}{s\sqrt{t}}$$

$$d_2 = d_1 - s\sqrt{t}$$

$$Q_p = Q_c - S + Ee^{-rt}$$

Where Q_c = call option value

Q_p = put option value

S = current stock price

E = exercise price

N(d) = cumulative normal density function

t = time until expiration

e = 2.7182818

r = risk free interest rate

s = standard deviation of stock returns

of index volatility suggests that estimation of future volatility will be difficult.

The most straightforward way to estimate volatility is to calculate the standard deviation of historical index price (closing level) changes as follows:

$$\text{standard deviation} = S = \sqrt{ \overline{X} \{(X_1 - \overline{X})^2 + (X_2 - \overline{X})^2 + ... + (X_n - \overline{X})^2 / N-1\} }$$

where
X_n = index closing level for time n
$\overline{X}$ = average index closing level for the historical series
N = number of observations in series

Historical closing levels for optionable indexes can be obtained by writing the exchanges (see Appendix D).

The volatility calculated in this way should be annualized for use in the Black-Scholes computation. For example, if weekly closing index levels are used, the standard deviation should be multiplied by the square root of 52. If daily closing index levels are used, the calculated volatility should be multiplied by the square root of the number of trading days in the year, or about 250. The number of historical observations which should be used is a matter of debate. However, long run volatility may be more appropriate to long term investment programs while short run volatility may be more appropriate to short term programs.

Dividend Adjustment

Because dividends have a negative impact on option prices, the omission of dividends from the Black-Scholes computation results in slightly inflated call prices. This price inflation will be greater for indexes that pay higher aggregate dividends. To account for dividends the following procedure can be employed with a high degree of accuracy. Decrease the stock price by the present value of the dividends likely to be paid prior to the option's maturity. Because the dividend stream on a broad-based index is spread over the entire year, a constant dividend yield is a good estimation of the actual dividend stream. Then calculate the option price using the traditional Black-Scholes formula.

Sample Black-Scholes Computation

An example using the model to solve for the price of an option is shown in Exhibit 7-5. The option selected for evaluation is the SPX September 310 call from August 24, 1990, first shown in Exhibit 4-1. The market price of the call can be observed in Chapter 4 as 11; however, the Black-Scholes computation shows a theoretical price of 7.6. How can the difference be accounted for?

The answer lies in the volatility input to the model. Recall that index volatility over the life of the option is difficult to estimate and has positive impact on call prices. The sample computation uses 18% volatility (the approximate volatility of the S&P 500 during 1990) while the market is clearly utilizing much higher expected volatility to compute the option value. In fact, sensitivity analysis reveals that a volatility input of 28% will result in a Black-Scholes theoretical value of 11. The 28% volatility is called market implied volatility because it is the volatility implicit in the market pricing of the option.

The implied volatility associated with this option price was unusually high relative to historically observed volatilities for the index. This was a result of the market uncertainty related to the crisis in the Middle East at that time—Iraq had invaded Kuwait only weeks earlier on August 2. Option writers at that time were demanding very high time value premiums to compensate for that uncertainty.

PRACTICAL IMPLICATIONS

Performing this exercise focuses attention on the difficulty in obtaining a fair value for options and establishing the true degree to which the market is undervaluing or overvaluing a particular issue. Unfortunately, the Black-Scholes model, while elegant in its simplicity, is deceptive in that some of the inputs to the equation are difficult to establish with the precision that is implied by the mathematics.

EXHIBIT 7-5

Sample Black-Scholes Computation

Data Inputs

Option:	SPX Sep 310 Call
Evaluation Date:	8-24-90
Index Level:	311.51
Dividend Yield:	3.5%
Div. Adj. Index Level:	310.65
Exercise Price:	310
Time to Expiration:	0.07945 years (29 days)
90-Day T-Bill	0.0769 (7.69%)
Index Volatility	0.18 (18%)

Calculation for Dividend Adjustment

$$PV = \frac{(0.035)\,(0.07945)\,(311.51)}{(1 + 0.0769)^{0.07945}}$$

$$= \frac{0.87}{1.01}$$

$$= 0.86$$

EXHIBIT 7-5 (Continued)

Sample Black-Scholes Computation

Calculation for d_1, d_2, $N(d_1)$, $N(d_2)$

$$d^1 = \frac{\ln\left(\frac{310.65}{310.00}\right) + \left[0.0769 + \frac{(0.18)^2}{2} \right](0.07945)}{0.18\sqrt{0.07945}}$$

$$= 0.1871$$

$$d_2 = 0.1871 - 0.18\sqrt{0.07945}$$

$$= 0.1364$$

$$N(d_1)^* = 0.5742$$

$$N(d_2)^* = 0.5543$$

Calculation for Call Option Value

$$Q_c = (310.65)(0.5742) - (310)(0.5543)e^{-(0.0769)(0.07945)}$$

$$= 178.38 \quad - \quad 170.78$$

$$= 7.6$$

* Methods for determining N(d) are provided in Appendix G.

Dividend Uncertainty

There is always some uncertainty surrounding the magnitude of the stock dividend. For most indexes, the quarterly dividend yield is easily identified from historical patterns. However, the dividend yield is not assured and changes occur as the index price level fluctuates. Possible changes would be reflected partially—but not fully—in the price of the traded option.

Simultaneous Trade Uncertainty

Trading in options is not necessarily active and continuous. The index price may meander without accompanying option trades at each price level. Thus, there may not be simultaneity in reported index and option prices. Based on last sale prices, options may seem cheap or dear. However, investors seeking to exploit perceived mispricing may find that business cannot necessarily be transacted at these prices.

Volatility Uncertainty

The index volatility is the input most subject to uncertainty. Unfortunately, it is the parameter to which the model is most sensitive. While the calculation for volatility is precise, it is backward looking. Ideally, the volatility would be that value which prevailed during the life of the option. Volatility of indexes has been historically unstable and is subject to variation based on a number of factors including sentiment, market fundamentals and index price level.

Some market observers determine the market's assessment of current volatility by using the Black-Scholes equation. The quoted option price is assumed to be the "correct" price, and the model is then used to determine which value of volatility gives that option value—the implied market volatility.

LOOKING AHEAD

This concludes the examination of index option valuation. Chapter 8 will build upon the information presented thus far to demonstrate a simple method of index option replication.

8

Index Option
Replication

Chapter 5 demonstrated that certain combinations of securities result in net profit profiles that resemble individual option profiles. This observation is the precursor to the present chapter on index option replication. Further, Chapter 7 demonstrated the dynamic nature of an option profit profile during its life. The discussion showed that even if intrinsic value is constant, total value will vary over the life of the option as the time value premium erodes due to the passage of time. Therefore, in order to replicate a profit profile over the life of an option, investors must have a strategy that is also dynamically responsive to the passage of time. This chapter describes one mechanism for artificially creating the profit profile for a long call option. This strategy mimics the dynamic call option profile without the use of actual options. The technique is useful because in certain situations an option-like profit profile may be desirable while the use of actual options is not. Examples include situations in which the options are deemed too expensive, risky, or unavailable.

OPTION DELTA

One of the important by-products of the Black-Scholes formula is the precise computation of the option delta. Option delta is defined as

EXHIBIT 8-1

Option Delta

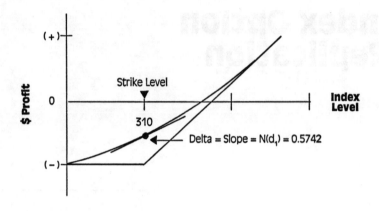

the dollar amount by which the option price will change for a one dollar change in the underlying index. In the Black-Scholes formula, the delta is equal to the $N(d_1)$ term. Delta is important because it is a measure of the option's exposure to changes in the underlying index. An illustration may make this point clearer.

Recall the sample Black-Scholes computation from Chapter 7. The computation was performed on an SPX September 310 call with an $N(d_1)$ of 0.5742. This call option is represented in Exhibit 8-1.

The exhibit shows two profiles: the profile at expiration that reflects only intrinsic value and the profile on the evaluation date that reflects intrinsic value plus time value premium. Both profiles show that the value of the option depends upon the value of the underlying index. However, the sensitivities of the option values to changes in the underlying are clearly different. Delta is a measure of this sensitivity. It is equal to the slope of the line tangent to the point along the profile at which the option currently resides:

$$\text{delta} = N(d_1) = \text{change in option price}/\text{change in underlying index price}$$

Exhibit 8-1 shows that when the index equals 310 the delta of the option on the evaluation date is 0.57. This means that a one point upward (downward) move in the index causes the option value to increase (decrease) by about 0.57 point. By contrast, the value of the option at expiration moves one for one with the underlying index (delta=1) at index levels greater than 310, and is completely insensitive to changes in the underlying index (delta=0) when the index level is less than 310.

For options with curved profit profiles (i.e., options with long times to expiration) the delta is a good sensitivity measure for small movements in the underlying index only. This is because delta is the slope of a straight line that seeks to describe the behavior of a curved profile. If the market moves substantially, the option will reside at a new and distant point along the profile. The delta must be recalculated to realign it to the correct portion of the curve.

INDEX OPTION REPLICATION

Assume that the call shown in Exhibit 8-1 is the option that the investor seeks to replicate. The exhibit shows that with the index at about 310, the investor seeks to hold a current portfolio with a delta of about 0.57. For small changes in the underlying index, such a portfolio would respond with the same sensitivity as the call option being replicated. This portfolio can be constructed by using the delta as an allocation ratio for dividing the investor's portfolio between stocks and cash. If 57% of the investor's assets are kept in the S&P 500 while the remaining 43% of the investor's assets are shifted to money market, the replication is achieved for small changes in the underlying index. It is intuitively apparent that if 57% of a portfolio has a delta of 1 and 43% of a portfolio has delta of 0, the overall portfolio delta (weighted average) is 0.57.

Consider the behavior of the delta allocated portfolio. If the index moves down 1% to a level of 307, the stock portion (57%) of the portfolio also moves down about 1%, while the money market portion (43%) is unaffected. The overall effect on the portfolio is a downward move of about 0.57%. The portfolio movement in relation to the un-

EXHIBIT 8-2

Performance of the Delta Allocated Portfolio

	Index	Portfolio	=	Stock	+	Cash
Initial	310	62,000	=	62,000	+	0
Delta Allocated		62,000	=	35,340	+	26,660
After Decline	307	61,647	=	34,987	+	26,660

Index Decline	=	(310-307)/310	=	1.00%
Portfolio Decline	=	(62000-61647)/62000	=	0.57%

derlying index is similar to the movement of the desired call option. Exhibit 8-2 demonstrates this numerically.

Two things occur over the life of the hedge which will change the delta, and hence the appropriate allocation of funds. First is the passage of time. As the time value premium of the option decays, the delta will change with the shape of the profile. Second is the movement of the market. Recall that the delta is the slope of a straight line which seeks to describe the behavior of a curved profile. If the market moves substantially, the delta must be recalculated to realign it to the correct portion of the curve. The delta always represents the correct proportion of portfolio assets to invest in underlying index.

The change in the delta necessitates that the investor rebalance the portfolio periodically over the life of the program. Because it requires periodic rebalancing, this strategy is known as a dynamic option strategy. Institutional investors employing this strategy might rebalance weekly or even daily. In fact, the strategy works fairly well with much less frequent rebalancing. A six-month replication program might call for monthly rebalancing; a ten-year replication program might call for semi-annual rebalancing.

LOOKING AHEAD

This concludes the examination of index option replication and the conceptual development of stock index options as an investing vehicle. Chapter 9 will touch upon issues for special consideration prior to trading stock index options.

9

Special Considerations

Throughout this book, a sense of the real world has been incorporated by using actual options quotes from the newspaper and current world events to drive market outlook and investment strategy. However, to retain simplicity of presentation, the foregoing discussion and examples ignore several important considerations which should be addressed by any serious investor in stock index options. These topics are important because they impact the final profit and/or loss profiles that investors will experience through trading in stock index options. As before, information that is of greatest practical value is emphasized. For more detailed discussions of these topics the reader is referred to the bibliography at the end of this book.

MARGIN REQUIREMENTS

You may recall from Chapter 4 that the seller of an option stands opposite the buyer ready to fulfill the obligations of the option contract upon demand. In consideration for this readiness, the seller receives the option premium. However, what ensures that the seller will be financially prepared to perform on an options contract should the need arise? The answer is that the exchange requires sellers of

EXHIBIT 9-1

Position	Margin Requirement	Calculation	Margin*
Short OEX Sep 305 Call @ 5 5/8 S&P 100 = 296	Option premium plus 15% of the underlying index less the amount by which the option is out of the money, or premium plus 10% of underlying index, whichever is greater.	option premium = 562.5 15% of underlying index = 4,440 out-of-money amount = 900 10 % of underlying index = 2,960	4,102.50 vs 3,522.5 therefore: $4,102.5
Short OEX Sep 290 Put @ 7 3/4 S&P 100 = 296	Option premium plus 15% of the underlying index less the amount by which the option is out of the money, or premium plus 10% of underlying index, whichever is greater.	option premium = 775 15% of underlying index = 4,440 out-of-money amount = 600 10 % of underlying index = 2,960	4,615 vs 3,735 therefore: $4,615

* All new transactions and subsequent commitments in a margin account must result in a minimum equity in the account of $2,000. Margin requirement may be reduced by the net option proceeds.

index options to produce *margin* (a deposit of cash or securities) as an indication of financial ability. Margin is held by the broker until the seller's position expires or is sold.

Margin requirements for stock index options vary. Generally, the requirements for broad-based indexes are less strict than those for narrow-based ones because the narrow-based indexes are more volatile. Investors should familiarize themselves with the margin requirements of any specific option prior to trading it. These requirements are detailed in the contract specifications in Appendix C. The following examples demonstrate the procedure for calculation of initial minimum exchange required margin for several options strategies.

EXHIBIT 9-2

Position	Margin Requirement	Calculation	Margin*
Long 4 XAU Sep 120 Calls @ 4 3/4	The difference between the purchase cost of the long call and the proceeds from the short call.	long call cost = 1,900 short call proceeds = 1,100	$800
Short 4 XAU Sep 125 Calls @ 2 3/4			

* All new transactions and subsequent commitments in a margin account must result in a minimum equity in the account of $2,000.

Individual Calls & Puts

Consider the writer of an option on the S&P 100 Index. Exhibit 9-1 displays calculation of minimum required margin for call or put writers on this option using closing index values and option prices from Chapter 5. As specified in the exhibit, the required margin for uncovered writers is *the dollar amount of the premium plus 15% of the underlying index value (index level times $100) less the amount by which the option is out of the money, or premium plus 10% of underlying index value, whichever is greater.*

Bull Spread

Recall the bull spread investor in the PHLX Gold & Silver Index in Chapter 5. Exhibit 9-2 displays calculation of minimum required margin for this investor. As specified in the exhibit, the required margin is *the difference between the purchase cost of the long call and the proceeds of the short call.*

Bear Spread

Recall the bear spread investor in the AMEX Oil Index in Chapter 5. Exhibit 9-3 displays calculation of minimum required margin

EXHIBIT 9-3

Position	Margin Requirement	Calculation	Margin*
Long 2 XOI Sep 265 Puts @ 8 7/8	The difference between the purchase cost of the long call and the proceeds from the short call.	long put cost = 1,775 short put proceeds = 550	$1,225
Short 2 XOI Sep 240 Calls @ 2 3/4			

* All new transactions and subsequent commitments in a margin account must result in a minimum equity in the account of $2,000.

EXHIBIT 9-4

Position	Margin Requirement	Calculation	Margin*
Short 2 OEX Sep 295 Calls @ 11 5/8 S&P 100 = 296	Short call or short put requirement, whichever is greater, plus any in-the-money amount of the other side.	short call requirement = 6,765 short put requirement = 6,240 short call in-money amount = 100 short put in-money amount = 0	$6,765
Short 2 OEX Sep 295 Puts @ 9 1/2 S&P 100 = 296			

* All new transactions and subsequent commitments in a margin account must result in a minimum equity in the account of $2,000. Margin requirment may be reduced by the net option proceeds.

for this investor. As specified in the exhibit, the required margin is *the difference between the purchase cost of the long put and the proceeds of the short put.*

Short Straddle

Recall the short straddle investor in the S&P 100 Index in Chapter 5. Exhibit 9-4 displays calculation of minimum required margin for this investor. As specified in the exhibit, the required margin is *the short call or short put requirement, whichever is greater, plus any in-the-money amount of the other side.*

TAXES

Although certain options transactions are subject to special and complex tax treatment, treatment of most stock index options transactions is straightforward. Unfortunately, even straightforward tax treatment can be confusing and tax laws are constantly changing. The following discussion outlines basic rules governing taxation of index options for individual investors. It is intended as a guide and is not exhaustive. Entities other than individuals may be subject to slightly different rules. Tax sensitive investors are encouraged to consult a tax advisor prior to trading.

Capital Gains & Losses

Because options are classified as capital assets, gains and losses generated through their use are treated as capital gains and losses. Prior to 1988, long-term capital gains enjoyed advantaged tax treatment. As a result, investors had tax-based incentives to hold investments for longer time horizons. However, the Tax Reform Act of 1986 generally eliminated preferential tax treatment of long-term capital gains over other forms of income beginning in 1988. Thus, beginning in 1988, long-term capital gains were taxed at the same rate as an individual's salary, interest and dividend income, and short-term capital gains.

Recently, however, the Reconciliation Tax Act of 1990 reinstated preferential tax treatment for long-term capital gains beginning in

1991. This advantaged tax treatment is available to certain investors because the 1990 Act fixes a maximum tax rate of 28% on net capital gains (defined as net long-term capital gains less net short-term capital losses). Unfortunately, other elements of the 1990 Act such as limitations on itemized deductions may result in an effective tax rate on net capital gains in excess of 28%. Further, the 1990 Act increased the alternative minimum tax rate from 21% to 24%, and this may also influence the desirability of holding profitable capital gains positions for extended time periods. Capturing the tax advantage afforded long-term capital gains under the 1990 Act is tricky and strategies designed to do so should be carefully devised.

Although capital losses can be used without limitation to offset capital gains, limitations do apply to their use to offset other forms of income. Currently, up to $3000 of ordinary income can be offset by capital loss (long-term or short-term) in any given year. For property acquired after December 31, 1987, the long-term holding period is generally considered to be more than one year. References to long-term holding periods in this discussion assume property acquired after December 31, 1987.

Mark-to-Market & the 60/40 Rule

Mark-to-market tax treatment requires that assets be valued at fair market value on the last business day of the taxable year, and treated as if sold (and repurchased) at fair value on that day for tax purposes. This treatment has the effect of forcing recognition of unrealized gains or losses on those assets for the current tax year, and establishes a new cost basis for the assets for the upcoming tax year. For assets which require mark-to-market treatment, all gains and losses actually realized—or deemed realized due to the mark-to-market procedure—are aggregated at year end.

After netting the combined gains and losses, the net gain or loss is subject to the 60/40 rule. This rule requires that the net gain or loss is treated as 60% long-term and 40% short-term, regardless of the actual holding period of the positions. The 60/40 rule is desirable because it enables certain investors to capture advantaged long term treatment for a portion of gains created from short term trading activity.

Net gains created in this way are treated as any other capital gains and can be offset by any other capital losses. Further, net gains become investment income for investment interest limitation purposes. Investment income limitation stipulates that an individual may deduct interest on debt incurred to purchase or carry investment property in an amount less than or equal to the individual's net investment income.

Eligibility

Technically, options on indexes that either (i) have been designated as eligible for trading on a commodity futures exchange by the Commodity Trading Futures Commission (CFTC), or (ii) have been determined as allowable for CFTC designation by the U.S. Treasury are eligible for 60/40 mark-to-market treatment. In practice, this means that 60/40 mark-to-market treatment applies to all broad-based U.S. stock index options (except those on the AMEX Japan Index) and to none of the narrow-based index options. Eligibility applies equally to holders of long and short options positions. Gain or loss on any index option position (eligible or ineligible) that either expires, is exercised, assigned, or sold prior to the last day of the taxable year is treated in conformance with the previous section on capital gains and losses, and 60/40 mark-to-market treatment is unnecessary.

COMMISSIONS

Commissions on stock index option transactions are typically calculated as a percentage of the cost of the options. This percentage is called the commission rate and generally declines as the dollar size of the transaction increases. In Chapter 5 it was mentioned that the commission rate at a discount broker should be about 2% of the cost of the options. In fact one might expect rates to range from about 3% on smaller transactions in the $2000 range to about 1.25% on larger transactions in the $10,000 range. Commission schedules are available upon request from discount and full service brokers. Investors should expect that full service brokerage rates will be substantially higher.

Although the commission rates for options may seem high compared to those on ordinary stock, options are actually cheaper to trade than stock in terms of dollar exposure obtained. Consider for example the investor from the protective put example from Chapter 5 who purchased two S&P 500 October 310 put options at a cost of $2650. These options hedged an underlying portfolio value of $62,000 at a commission cost of about $79. However, the purchase of $62,000 of common stock at an average stock price of $50 per share and a commission rate of $0.08 per share would cost about $99.

PRICE RETURN VS. TOTAL RETURN

When discussing stock returns, investors must distinguish between price return and total return. Price return refers only to the gain or loss associated with the change in price of the underlying securities. Total return refers to price return plus gains associated with the receipt of dividends. Therefore, if an investor held a stock which suffered a price decline of 10% but paid a dividend of 3.5%, the investor's total return would be − 6.5%.

From the discussion in Chapter 2, readers should understand that the indexes which underlie stock index options capture only the price component of total return. These indexes are called price indexes. In fact, most publishers of stock indexes maintain both price indexes and total return indexes. However, total return indexes are not applicable in the context of index options. Stock index options are always valued based upon the movement of the underlying price index.

The distinction between price return and total return has implications for investors in stock index options. For example, consider the investor from Chapter 5 who bought protective put options to hedge an underlying portfolio. The investor carefully calculated the appropriate number of options based on current portfolio value. If the investor received all portfolio dividends in cash (so that changes in portfolio value reflected only price return) the hedge would work as described in the example. However, if the investor reinvested dividend flow (so that changes in portfolio value reflected total return) the hedge would be slightly mismatched. The portfolio would always be slightly more valuable than anticipated in the analysis to reflect the amount of dividends reinvested. In practice, this mismatch is typically very small. However, hedgers must understand that index options can only hedge the price returns and not the total returns associated with an underlying portfolio. Similarly, speculators must understand that index options can only capture the price returns and not the total returns associated with designated markets.

Appendix A:
Optionable Indexes

American Stock Exchange Computer Technology Index

The AMEX Computer Technology Index is a narrow-based capitalization-weighted index of 30 widely held stocks representing various segments of the computer industry. This index is designed to measure U.S. computer industry performance through changes in the aggregate market value of 30 leading computer technology corporations. The index was developed with a benchmark value of 100 as of July 29, 1983. A list of component stocks and a chart of historical index movements follow.

AMEX Computer Technology Index—Component Stocks*

Advanced Micro Devices	Intel
Amdahl	Microsoft
Apple Computer	Motorola
Automatic Data Processing	National Semiconductor
Commodore International	NBI
COMPAQ Computer	NCR
Computer Sciences	Quantel
Control Data	Storage Technology
Cray Research	Sun Microsystems
Data General	Tandem Computers
Datapoint	Tandy
Digital Equipment	Texas Instruments
Hewlett-Packard	Unisys
Honeywell	Wang Laboratories, Cl. B
IBM	Xerox

*As of August 1989.

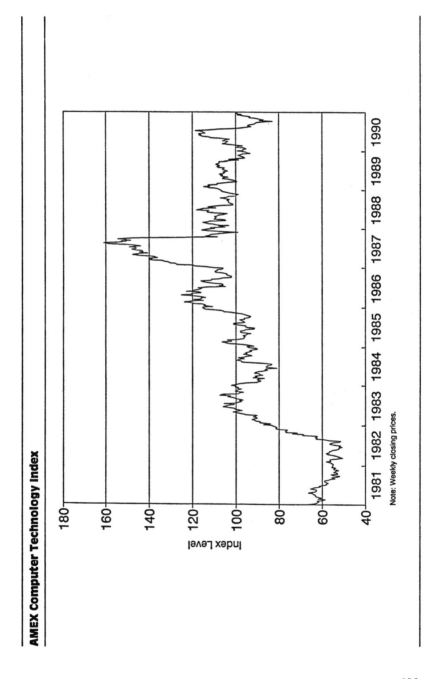

American Stock Exchange Institutional Index

The American Stock Exchange Institutional Index is a capitalization-weighted index of the 75 stocks currently held in the greatest dollar amounts among institutional equity portfolios. This index is designed to measure U.S. institutional investor performance through changes in the aggregate market value of core stock holdings of large scale institutional investors. The index was developed with a benchmark of 250 as of June 24, 1986. A list of component stocks and a chart of historical index movements follow.

American Stock Exchange Institutional Index—Component Stocks*

Abbott Laboratories	Emerson Electric	NYNEX
Aetna Life & Casualty	Exxon	Pacific Telesis
Aluminum Company of America	Federal National Mortgage Assoc.	J.C. Penney
American Express	Ford Motor	Pepsico
American Home Products	Gannett	Pfizer
American Information Technologies	General Electric	Philip Morris
American International Group	General Motors	Procter & Gamble
Amoco Corporation	General Re	Royal Dutch Petroleum
Anheuser Busch	GTE	Schering Plough
AT&T	H.J. Heinz	Schlumberger
Atlantic Richfield	Hewlett-Packard	Sears, Roebuck
Bell Atlantic	IBM	Southwestern Bell
BellSouth	Intel	Tenneco
Boeing	Johnson & Johnson	Texaco
Bristol-Meyers Squibb	Kellogg	Toys R Us
Chevron	KMart	Union Pacific
Citicorp	Eli Lilly	United Technologies
Coca-Cola	Loews	United Telecommunications
Deere	MCI Communications	US WEST
Digital Equipment	McDonalds	USX
Disney	Merck	Wal-Mart Stores
Dow Chemical	Minnesota Mining & Manufacturing	Warner-Lambert
Dun & Bradstreet	Mobil	Waste Management
DuPont	Monsanto	Westinghouse Electric
Eastman Kodak	J.P. Morgan	
	Motorola	

*As of June 1990 based on institutional holdings as of March 1990.

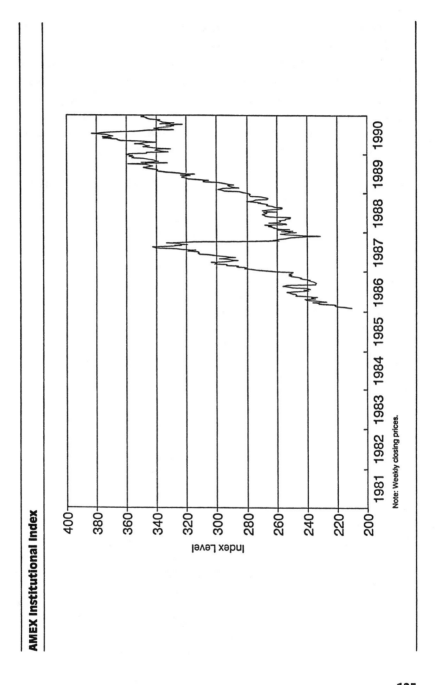

AMEX Institutional Index

Index Level

Note: Weekly closing prices.

American Stock Exchange International Market Index

The American Stock Exchange International Market Index is a capitalization-weighted index of 50 leading foreign stocks from 10 countries and 20 industry groups. This index is designed to measure economic performance of non-U.S. industrialized world regions including Europe, Australia, and the Far East. The index was developed with a benchmark of 200 as of January 2, 1987. A list of component stocks and a chart of historical index movements follow.

American Stock Exchange International Market Index—Component Stocks*

ASEA AB	Mitsubishi Bank Limited
Banco Central SA	Matsushita Electric Industries
Barclays PLC ADS	Montedison SPA
Broken Hill Properties	National Australia Bank
British Petroleum	Norsk Hydro AS
B.A.T. Indurstries PLC	NEC
Burmah Oil PLC	Norsk Data AS
Cadbury Schweppes PLC	Nissan Motor
Canon	Novo Industries AS
Dresdner Bank AG	National Westminster PLC
Empresa Nacional de Electricidad	News Corp.
Elan	Pacific Dunlop Limited
Electrolux AB	Philips NV
Ericsson Telephone	Rank Organisation PLC
Fisons PLC	Royal Dutch Petroleum
Fuji Photo Film	Reuters Holdings PLC
Glaxo PLC	Saatchi & Saatchi
Hanson Trust PLC	Smithkline Beecham PLC
Hitachi Limited	Sony
Hong Kong Telecom	TDK
Honda Motor Co ADS	Compania de Telef Nac
Imperial Chemical Industries	Tokio Marine & Fire
Ito-Yokado	Toyota Motor
KLM Royal Dutch Air	Unilever NV
Kyocera	Volvo AB

*As of June 1990.

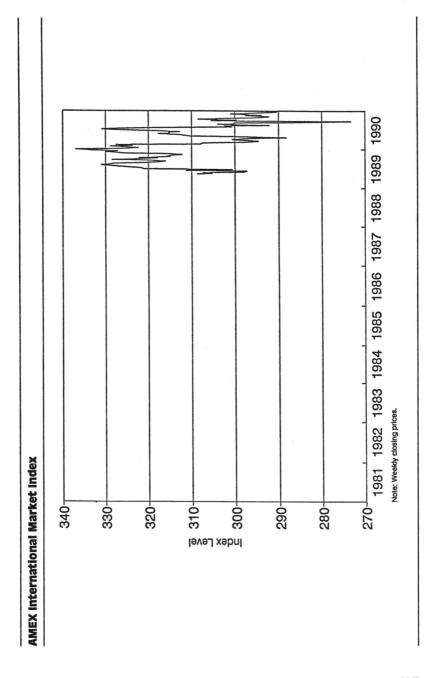

AMEX International Market Index

Note: Weekly closing prices.

127

American Stock Exchange Japan Index

The American Stock Exchange Japan Index is a modified price-weighted index of 210 common stocks actively traded on the Tokyo Stock Exchange. This index is designed to measure economic performance of the overall Japanese economy through changes in the aggregate price level of a broad cross section of Japanese corporations. The index is denominated in U.S. dollars. The modified price weighting calculation ensures that changes in index level reflect only price changes of component stocks and not currency fluctuations. The index was developed with a benchmark of 280 as of April 2, 1990. A list of component industry groups and a chart of historical index movements follow.

Japan Index—Component Industry Groups*

Air Transportation	Iron & Steel	Retail Stores
Banking	Machinery	Rubber Products
Chemicals	Marine Products	Sea Transport
Clay & Glass	Metal Products	Securities/Finance
Communications	Mining	Services
Construction	Motor Vehicles	Shipbuilding
Drugs	Other Manufacturing	Textile Production
Electric Equipment	Paper & Pulp	Trade
Electric Power	Petroleum	Transport Equipment
Food	Precision Instruments	Trucking
Gas Services	Railroad Transportation	Warehousing
Insurance	Real Estate	

*As of September 21, 1990.

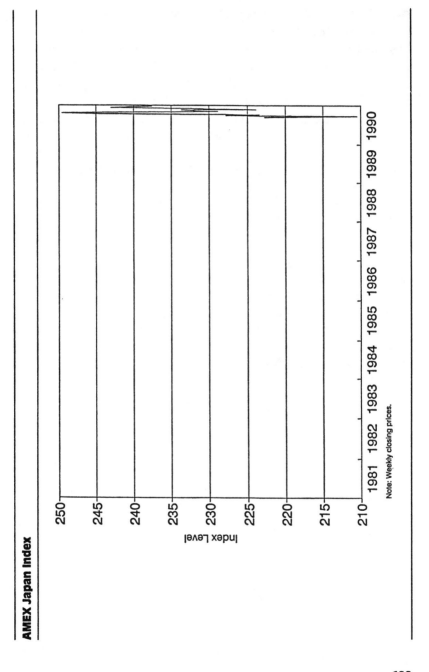

AMEX Japan Index

Index Level

250 245 240 235 230 225 220 215 210

1981 1982 1983 1984 1985 1986 1987 1988 1989 1990

Note: Weekly closing prices.

129

American Stock Exchange Major Market Index

The American Stock Exchange Major Market Index is a price weighted arithmetic average of 20 major blue chip stocks representative of major US industrial corporations. This index is designed to measure performance of dominant U.S. industrial corporations by mirroring the movements of the Dow Jones Industrial Average. Because it is calculated as an average, the index has no base value. A list of component stocks and a chart of historical index movements follow.

American Stock Exchange Major Market Index—Component Stocks*

American Express	IBM
AT&T	International Paper
Chevron	Johnson & Johnson
Coca-Cola	Merck
Dow Chemical	Minnesota Mining
Du Pont	Mobil
Eastman Kodak	Philip Morris
Exxon	Procter & Gamble
General Electric	Sears, Roebuck
General Motors	USX

*As of February 1989.

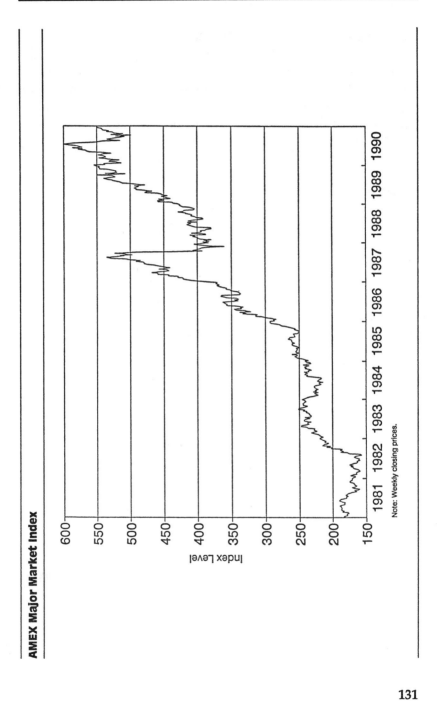

AMEX Major Market Index

Index Level

600 550 500 450 400 350 300 250 200 150

1981 1982 1983 1984 1985 1986 1987 1988 1989 1990

Note: Weekly closing prices.

American Stock Exchange Oil Index

The American Stock Exchange Oil Index is a price-weighted index of 16 widely held stocks representing various segments of the oil industry. This index is designed to measure U.S. oil industry performance through changes in the aggregate price level of stocks from 16 leading oil industry corporations. The index was developed with a benchmark of 125 as of August 27, 1984. A list of component stocks and a chart of historical index movements follow.

American Stock Exchange Oil Index—Component Stocks*

Amerada Hess	Mobil
Amoco	Occidental Petroleum
Atlantic Richfield	Oryx Energy
British Petroleum Company PLC	Phillips Petroleum
Chevron	Royal Dutch Petroleum
Du Pont	Sun Company
Exxon	Texaco
Kerr-McGee	Unocal

*As of February 1990.

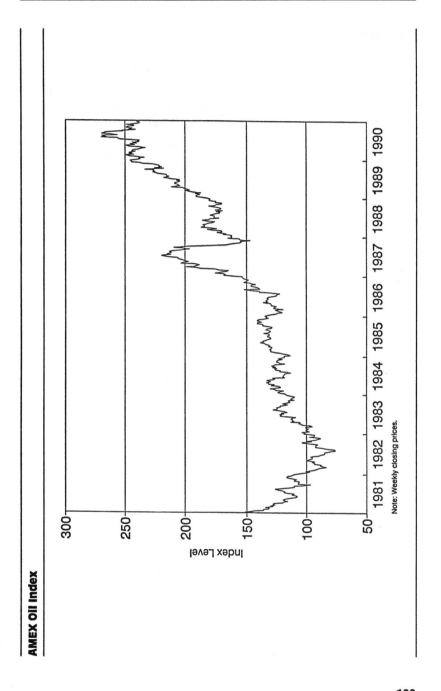

AMEX Oil Index

Index Level

300   250   200   150   100   50

1981 1982 1983 1984 1985 1986 1987 1988 1989 1990

Note: Weekly closing prices.

Financial News Composite Index

The Financial News Composite Index is a price-weighted index of 30 large capitalization stocks listed on the New York Stock Exchange. This index is designed to measure performance of the dominant U.S. industrial economy through changes in the aggregate price level of 20 blue chip domestic corporations. The FNC Index is intended to mirror the movements of the Dow Jones Industrial Average. A list of component stocks and a chart of historical index movements follow.

Financial News Composite Index—Component Stocks*

Aetna Life & Casualty	Eastman Kodak
Allied Signal Inc.	Exxon
Aluminum Company of America	General Electric
American Express	General Motors
American Home Products	Goodyear Tire & Rubber
AT&T	Heinz
BellSouth	IBM
Boeing	International Paper
CitiCorp	Merck
Coca-Cola	Merrill Lynch
CSX	Minnesota Mining & Manufacturing
Delta Air Lines	Philip Morris
Digital Equipment	Schlumberger
Disney	SCE
Dow Chemical	Sears, Roebuck

*As of February 1990.

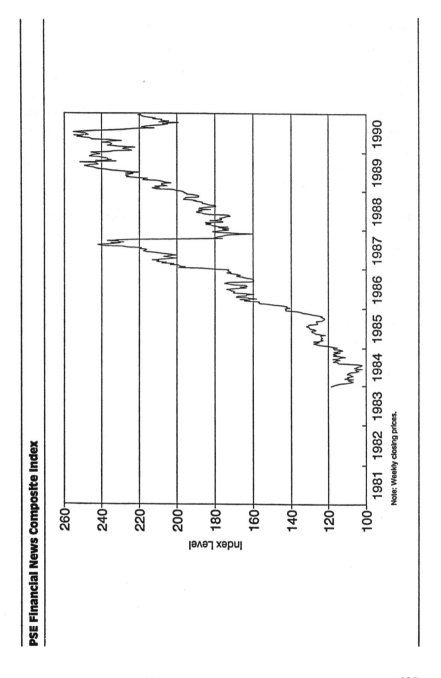

PSE Financial News Composite Index

Index Level

260 240 220 200 180 160 140 120 100

1981 1982 1983 1984 1985 1986 1987 1988 1989 1990

Note: Weekly closing prices.

New York Stock Exchange Composite Index

The New York Stock Exchange Composite Index is a capitalization-weighted index of all 1600+ common stocks listed on the New York Stock Exchange. This index is designed to measure performance of the whole NYSE through changes in the aggregate market value of all companies listed on the exchange. The index was developed with a benchmark value of 50 as of December 31, 1965. With a base value of 50, the NYSE composite has the distinction of being the optionable index with the lowest price level. A list of component stocks and a chart of historical index movements follow.

New York Stock Exchange Composite Index—Top Ten Component Stocks*

IBM
Exxon
General Electric
General Motors
Shell Oil
Standard Oil of Indiana
Schlumberger
AT&T
Mobil
Standard Oil of California

*As of March 30, 1984.

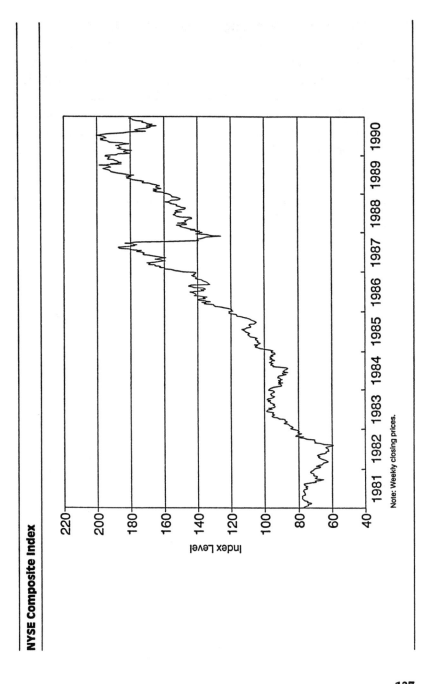

NYSE Composite Index

Index Level

220 200 180 160 140 120 100 80 60 40

1981 1982 1983 1984 1985 1986 1987 1988 1989 1990

Note: Weekly closing prices.

Philadelphia Stock Exchange Gold & Silver Index

The Philadelphia Stock Exchange Gold & Silver Index is a capitalization-weighted index of 7 companies involved in gold and silver mining and production. This index is designed to measure the performance of the U.S. gold and silver mining industry through changes in the aggregate market value of 7 dominant gold and silver industry corporations. The index was developed with a benchmark value of 100 as of December 19, 1983. A list of component stocks and a chart of historical index movements follow.

Philadelphia Stock Exchange Gold & Silver Index—Component Stocks*

ASA Limited
Battle Mountain Gold Co.
Echo Bay Mines Limited
Hecla Mining Company
Homestake Mining Company
Newmont Mining Corporation
Placer Dome Incorporated

*As of June 1990.

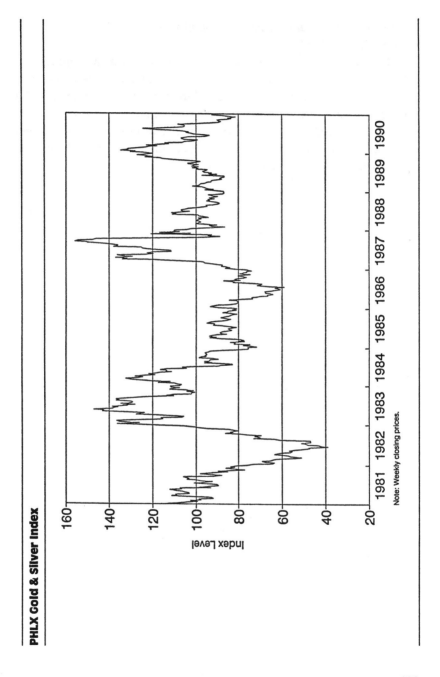

PHLX Gold & Silver Index

Note: Weekly closing prices.

Philadelphia Stock Exchange National Over-the-Counter Index

The Philadelphia Stock Exchange National Over-the-Counter Index is a capitalization-weighted index of the 100 largest over-the-counter stocks. This index is designed to measure performance of the broad domestic over-the-counter market by mirroring the movements of the NASDAQ-OTC Composite Index. The index was developed with a benchmark value of 150 as of September 28, 1984. A chart of historical index movements follows.

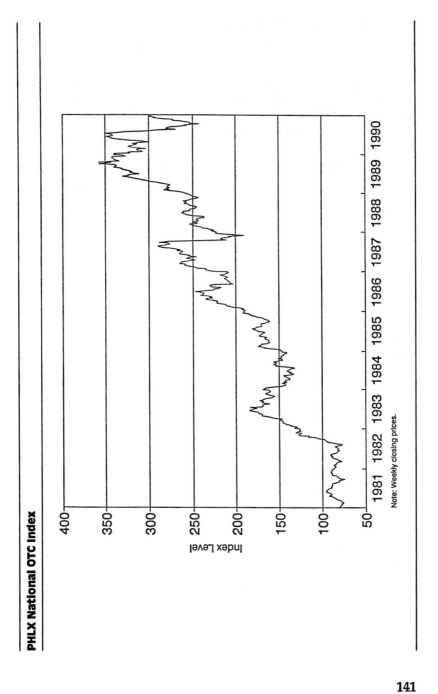

PHLX National OTC Index

Index Level

Note: Weekly closing prices.

1981 1982 1983 1984 1985 1986 1987 1988 1989 1990

Philadelphia Stock Exchange Utility Index

The Philadelphia Stock Exchange Utility Index is a capitalization-weighted index of 20 geographically diverse utility companies. This index is designed to measure the performance of the U.S. utility industry through changes in the aggregate market value of 20 dominant utility industry corporations. A list of component stocks and a chart of historical index movements follow.

Philadelphia Stock Exchange Utility Index—Component Stocks*

American Electric Power
Centerior Energy
Commonwealth Edison
Consolidated Edison Company of New York
Detroit Edison
Dominion Resources
Duke Power
FPL Group
Houston Industries
Niagara Mohawk Power
Northeast Utilities
Ohio Edison
Pacific Gas & Electric
PacifiCorp
Philadelphia Electric
Public Service Enterprise Group
SCE
Southern Company
Texas Utilities
Union Electric

*As of April 1990.

PHLX Utility Index

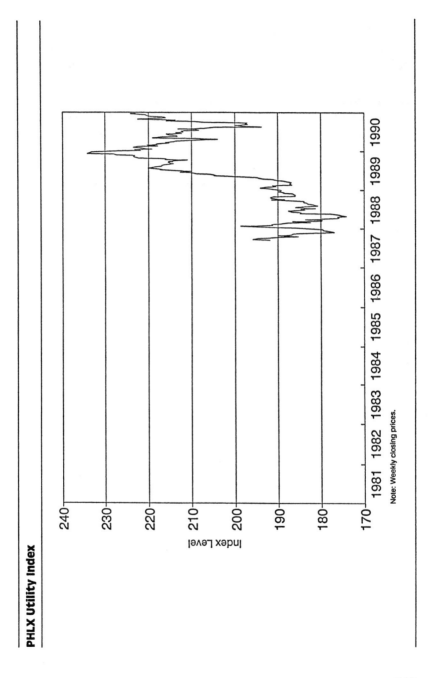

Note: Weekly closing prices.

143

Standard & Poor's 100 Index

The Standard & Poors 100 Index is a capitalization-weighted index of 100 stocks from a broad range of industries. This index is designed to measure performance of the broad domestic economy through changes in the aggregate market value of 100 stocks for which options are currently listed on the CBOE. The index was developed with a benchmark value of 100 as of January 2, 1976. A list of component stocks and a chart of historical index movements follow.

S&P 100 Index—Top Twenty-Five Component Stocks*

IBM	Atlantic Richfield
Exxon	Bell Atlantic
General Electric	PepsiCo
AT&T	Ameritech
Bristol-Meyers Squibb	Minnesota Mining & Manufacturing
Merck	Boeing
Wal-Mart Stores	Ford Motor
Coca-Cola	American International Group
Amoco	Schlumberger
Du Pont	Eastman Kodak
Mobil	Disney
General Motors	Dow Chemical
Johnson & Johnson	

*As of October 1990.

144

S&P 100 Index

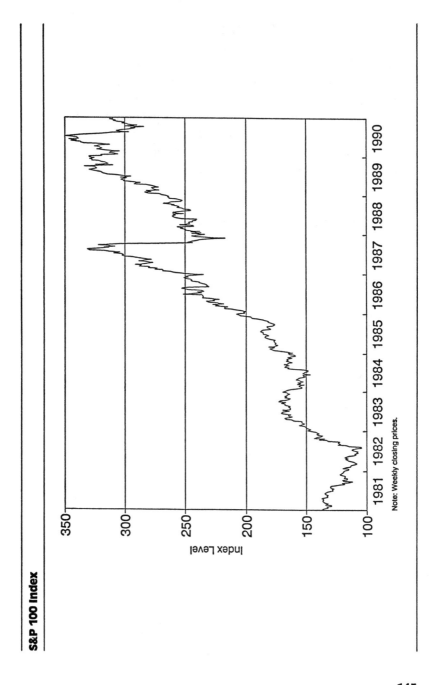

Note: Weekly closing prices.

Standard & Poor's 500 Index

The Standard & Poors 500 Index is a capitalization-weighted index of 500 stocks from a broad range of industries. This index is designed to measure performance of the broad domestic economy through changes in the aggregate market value of 500 stocks representing all major industries in approximately the same proportion to their representation on the New York Stock Exchange. The index was developed with a benchmark value of 10 based on aggregate stock values between 1941 and 1943. A list of component stocks and a chart of historical index movements follow.

S&P 500 Index—Top Twenty-Five Component Stocks*

IBM	Chevron
Exxon	Du Pont
General Electric	Mobil
Phillip Morris	General Motors
Royal Dutch Petroleum	Johnson & Johnson
AT&T	Atlantic Richfield
Bristol-Meyers Squibb	Lilly
Merck	Bell Atlantic
Wal-Mart Stores	PepsiCo
Coca-Cola	Abbott Labs
Proctor & Gamble	GTE
Amoco	Pacific Telesis
BellSouth	

*As of October 1990.

S&P 500 Index

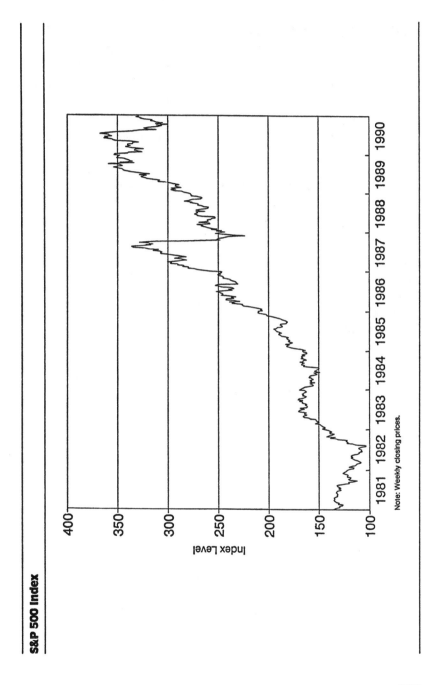

Note: Weekly closing prices.

Value Line Composite Index

The Value Line Composite Index is a price-weighted index of all stocks followed by the Value Line Investment Survey. This index is designed to measure performance of the whole Value Line universe through changes in the aggregate market value of all 1700+ stocks followed by the Survey. The index was developed with a benchmark value of 100 as of June 30, 1961. A list of component industry groups and a chart of historical index movements follow.

Value Line Composite Index—Top Ten Component Industry Groups*

Electric utility
Petroleum, oilfield services
Building
Retail stores, grocery
Consumer products, durables
Banks, savings & loans
Machinery
Electrical equipment
Computer
Transportation

*As of June 1987.

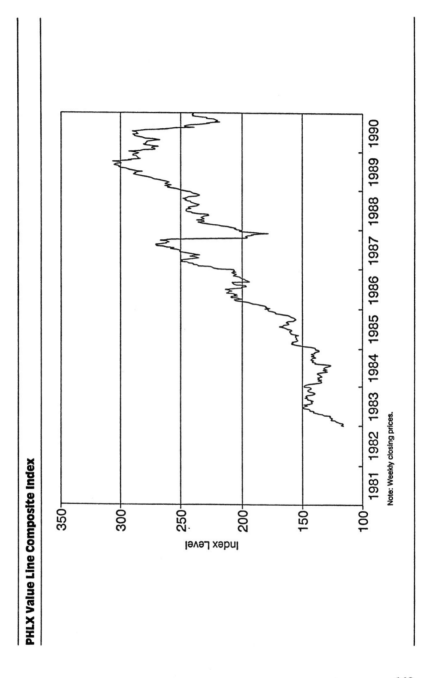

PHLX Value Line Composite Index

Index Level

Note: Weekly closing prices.

Appendix B:
Non-Optionable
Indexes

Dow Jones Industrial Average

The Dow Jones Industrial Average is a price-weighted arithmetic average of 30 high quality stocks compiled and published by the *Wall Street Journal* and its sister publication *Barron's National Business & Financial Weekly*. This index is designed to measure performance of dominant U.S. industrial corporations through changes in the aggregate price level of 30 blue chip domestic corporations. Because it is calculated as an average, the index has no base value. A list of component stocks and a chart of historical index movements follow.

Dow Jones Industrial Average—Component Stocks*

Allied Signal	International Paper
Alcoa	McDonalds
American Express	Merck
AT&T	Minnesota Mining & Manufacturing
Bethlehem Steel	Navistar
Boeing	Pillip Morris
Chevron	Primerica
Coca-Cola	Proctor & Gamble
Du Pont	Sears, Roebuck
Eastman Kodak	Texaco
Exxon	USX
General Electric	Union Carbide
General Motors	United Technologies
Goodyear	Westinghouse
IBM	Woolworth

*As of November 1990.

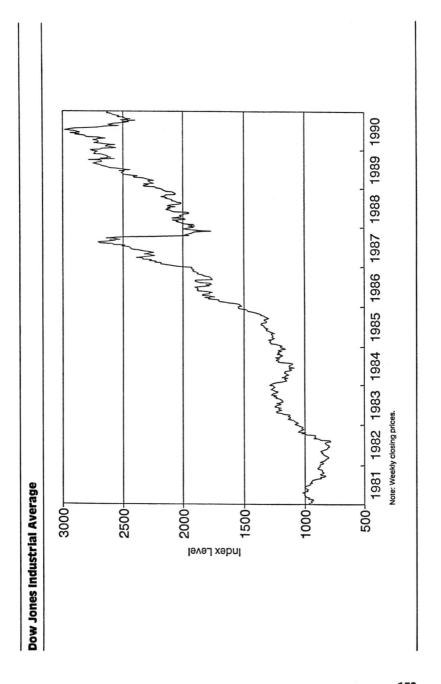

Dow Jones Industrial Average

Note: Weekly closing prices.

153

NASDAQ-OTC Composite Index

The NASDAQ-OTC Composite Index is a capitalization-weighted index of all over-the-counter stocks listed on the the National Association of Securities Dealers Automated Quotation system. This index is designed to measure performance of the broad, domestic over-the-counter market through changes in the aggregate market value of all 3600+ NASDAQ common stocks. The index was developed with a benchmark value of 100 as of February 5, 1971. A list of component stocks and a chart of historical index movements follow.

NASDAQ-OTC Composite Index—Top Ten Component Stocks*

Intel
American International Group
MCI
Berkshire Hathaway
Apple Computer
Farmers Group
Tandem Computers
Roadway Services
The St. Paul Companies
PACCAR

*As of December 31,1983.

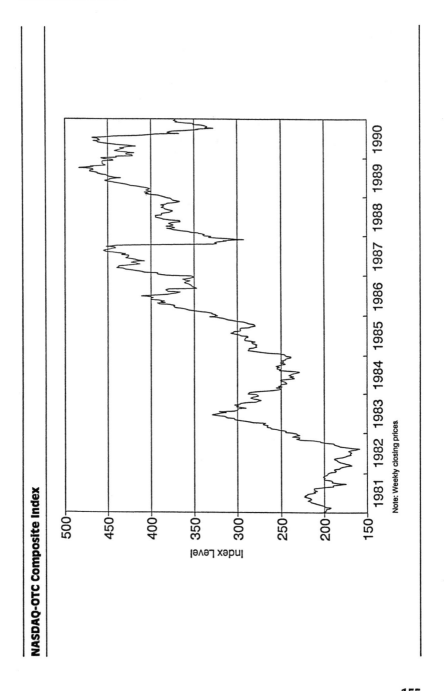

NASDAQ-OTC Composite Index

Note: Weekly closing prices.

155

Wilshire 5000 Equity Index

The Wilshire 5000 Equity Index is a capitalization-weighted index of all 5000+ actively traded common stocks in the United States. This index is designed to measure performance of the U.S. economy in the broadest possible sense through changes in the aggregate market value of all 5000+ actively traded common stocks. The index was developed with a benchmark value of 1404.6 as of December 31, 1980. A list of component stocks and a chart of historical index movements follow.

Wilshire 5000 Equity Index—Top Ten Component Stocks*

IBM
Exxon
General Electric
General Motors
Shell Oil
Standard Oil of Indiana
AT&T
Schlumberger
Gulf
Mobil

*As of March 22, 1984.

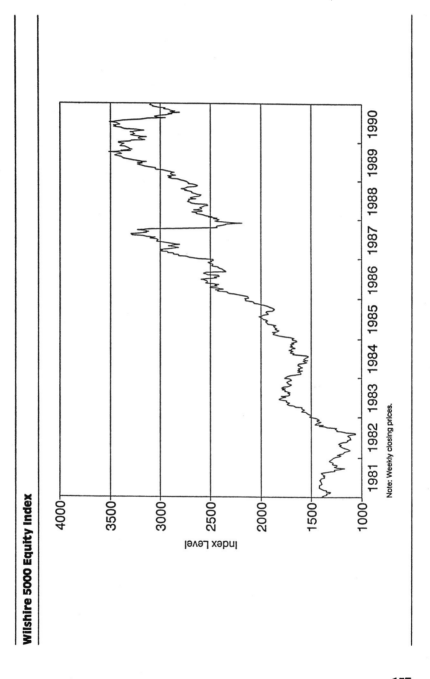

Wilshire 5000 Equity Index

Index Level

4000 3500 3000 2500 2000 1500 1000

1981 1982 1983 1984 1985 1986 1987 1988 1989 1990

Note: Weekly closing prices.

Appendix C:
Contract
Specifications

American Stock Exchange Computer Technology Index

EXCHANGE AMEX

SYMBOL XCI

CONTRACT MULTIPLIER 100

EXPIRATION CYCLE Monthly

EXPIRATION DATE
Saturday following third Friday of expiration month.

EXERCISE PRICES
Set at five-point intervals to bracket current index value. New exercise (strike) prices added as index moves.

PREMIUM QUOTATION
Expressed as points (and fractions thereof) where one point equals $100.

MARGIN REQUIREMENTS
Premium plus 20% of the underlying index value (index level times $100) less the amount by which the option is out-of-the-money, or premium plus 10% of underlying index value, whichever is greater.

EXERCISE SETTLEMENT
Cash settlement based on the dollar difference between the index level and the exercise price of the contract multiplied by 100. The index level is determined following the close of trading on the day exercise instructions are submitted.

EXERCISE PROCEDURE American.

TRADING HOURS 9:30 A.M. to 4:10 P.M. EST

American Stock Exchange Institutional Index

EXCHANGE AMEX

SYMBOL XII

CONTRACT MULTIPLIER 100

EXPIRATION CYCLE Monthly

EXPIRATION DATE
Saturday following third Friday of expiration month.

EXERCISE PRICES
Set at five-point intervals to bracket current index value. New exercise (strike) prices added as index moves.

PREMIUM QUOTATION
Expressed as points (and fractions thereof) where one point equals $100.

MARGIN REQUIREMENTS
Premium plus 15% of the underlying index value (index level times $100) less the amount by which the option is out-of-the-money, or premium plus 10% of underlying index value, whichever is greater.

EXERCISE SETTLEMENT
Cash settlement based on the dollar difference between the index level and the exercise price of the contract multiplied by 100. The index level is determined following the close of trading on the day exercise instructions are submitted.

EXERCISE PROCEDURE European.

TRADING HOURS 9:30 A.M. to 4:15 P.M. EST

American Stock Exchange International Market Index

EXCHANGE AMEX

SYMBOL ADR

CONTRACT MULTIPLIER 100

EXPIRATION CYCLE Monthly

EXPIRATION DATE
Saturday following third Friday of expiration month.

LAST TRADING DAY
Second to last business day before expiration.

EXERCISE PRICES
Set at five-point intervals to bracket current index value. New exercise (strike) prices added as index moves.

PREMIUM QUOTATION
Expressed as points (and fractions thereof) where one point equals $100.

MARGIN REQUIREMENTS
Premium plus 15% of the underlying index value (index level times $100) less the amount by which the option is out-of-the-money, or premium plus 10% of underlying index value, whichever is greater.

EXERCISE SETTLEMENT
Cash settlement based on the dollar difference between the index level and the exercise price of the contract multiplied by 100. The index level is determined following the close of trading on the day exercise instructions are submitted.

EXERCISE PROCEDURE European.

TRADING HOURS 9:30 A.M. to 4:15 P.M. EST

American Stock Exchange Japan Index

EXCHANGE AMEX

SYMBOL JPN

CONTRACT MULTIPLIER 100

EXPIRATION CYCLE Monthly

EXPIRATION DATE
Saturday following third Friday of expiration month.

LAST TRADING DAY
Second to last business day before expiration.

EXERCISE PRICES
Set at five-point intervals to bracket current index value. New exercise (strike) prices added as index moves.

PREMIUM QUOTATION
Expressed as points (and fractions thereof) where one point equals $100.

MARGIN REQUIREMENTS
Premium plus 15% of the underlying index value (index level times $100) less the amount by which the option is out-of-the-money, or premium plus 10% of underlying index value, whichever is greater.

EXERCISE SETTLEMENT
Cash settlement based on the dollar difference between the index level and the exercise price of the contract multiplied by 100. The index level is determined following the close of trading on the Tokyo Stock Exchange on the last business day in Japan prior to expiration.

EXERCISE PROCEDURE European.

TRADING HOURS 9:30 A.M. to 4:15 P.M. EST

American Stock Exchange Major Market Index

EXCHANGE AMEX

SYMBOL XMI

CONTRACT MULTIPLIER 100

EXPIRATION CYCLE Monthly

EXPIRATION DATE
Saturday following third Friday of expiration month.

EXERCISE PRICES
Set at five-point intervals to bracket current index value. New exercise (strike) prices added as index moves.

PREMIUM QUOTATION
Expressed as points (and fractions thereof) where one point equals $100.

MARGIN REQUIREMENTS
Premium plus 15% of the underlying index value (index level times $100) less the amount by which the option is out-of-the-money, or premium plus 10% of underlying index value, whichever is greater.

EXERCISE SETTLEMENT
Cash settlement based on the dollar difference between the index level and the exercise price of the contract multiplied by 100. The index level is determined following the close of trading on the day exercise instructions are submitted.

EXERCISE PROCEDURE European.

TRADING HOURS 9:30 A.M. to 4:15 P.M. EST

American Stock Exchange LT-20 Major Market Index

EXCHANGE AMEX

SYMBOL XLT

CONTRACT MULTIPLIER 100

EXPIRATION CYCLE Annually

EXPIRATION DATE
Saturday following third Friday of expiration month.

EXERCISE PRICES
Set at discretionary intervals to bracket current index value. New exercise (strike) prices added as index moves.

PREMIUM QUOTATION
Expressed as points (and fractions thereof) where one point equals $100.

MARGIN REQUIREMENTS
Premium plus 15% of the underlying index value (index level times $100) less the amount by which the option is out-of-the-money, or premium plus 10% of underlying index value, whichever is greater.

EXERCISE SETTLEMENT
Cash settlement based on the dollar difference between the index level and the exercise price of the contract multiplied by 100. The index level is determined following the close of trading on the day exercise instructions are submitted.

EXERCISE PROCEDURE European.

TRADING HOURS 9:30 A.M. to 4:15 P.M. EST

American Stock Exchange Oil Index

EXCHANGE AMEX

SYMBOL XOI

CONTRACT MULTIPLIER 100

EXPIRATION CYCLE Monthly

EXPIRATION DATE
Saturday following third Friday of expiration month.

EXERCISE PRICES
Set at five-point intervals to bracket current index value. New exercise (strike) prices added as index moves.

PREMIUM QUOTATION
Expressed as points (and fractions thereof) where one point equals $100.

MARGIN REQUIREMENTS
Premium plus 20% of the underlying index value (index level times $100) less the amount by which the option is out-of-the-money, or premium plus 10% of underlying index value, whichever is greater.

EXERCISE SETTLEMENT
Cash settlement based on the dollar difference between the index level and the exercise price of the contract multiplied by 100. The index level is determined following the close of trading on the day exercise instructions are submitted.

EXERCISE PROCEDURE American.

TRADING HOURS 9:30 A.M. to 4:10 P.M. EST

New York Stock Exchange Composite Index

EXCHANGE NYSE

SYMBOL NYA

CONTRACT MULTIPLIER 100

EXPIRATION CYCLE Monthly

EXPIRATION DATE
Saturday following third Friday of expiration month.

LAST TRADING DAY
Second to last business day before expiration.

EXERCISE PRICES
Set at two and one-half point intervals to bracket current index value. New exercise (strike) prices added as index moves.

PREMIUM QUOTATION
Expressed as points (and fractions thereof) where one point equals $100.

MARGIN REQUIREMENTS
Premium plus 15% of the underlying index value (index level times $100) less the amount by which the option is out-of-the-money, or premium plus 10% of underlying index value, whichever is greater.

EXERCISE SETTLEMENT
Cash settlement based on the dollar difference between the index level and the exercise price of the contract multiplied by 100. The index level is determined following the close of trading on the day exercise instructions are submitted.

EXERCISE PROCEDURE American.

TRADING HOURS 9:30 A.M. to 4:15 P.M. EST

Philadelphia Stock Exchange Gold & Silver Index

EXCHANGE PHLX

SYMBOL XAU

CONTRACT MULTIPLIER 100

EXPIRATION CYCLE Monthly

EXPIRATION DATE
Saturday following third Friday of expiration month.

EXERCISE PRICES
Set at five-point intervals to bracket current index value. New exercise (strike) prices added as index moves.

PREMIUM QUOTATION
Expressed as points (and fractions thereof) where one point equals $100.

MARGIN REQUIREMENTS
Premium plus 20% of the underlying index value (index level times $100) less the amount by which the option is out-of-the-money, or premium plus 10% of underlying index value, whichever is greater.

EXERCISE SETTLEMENT
Cash settlement based on the dollar difference between the index level and the exercise price of the contract multiplied by 100. The index level is determined following the close of trading on the day exercise instructions are submitted.

EXERCISE PROCEDURE American.

TRADING HOURS 9:30 A.M. to 4:10 P.M. EST

Philadelphia Stock Exchange National
Over-the-Counter Index

EXCHANGE PHLX

SYMBOL XOC

CONTRACT MULTIPLIER 100

EXPIRATION CYCLE Monthly

EXPIRATION DATE
Saturday following third Friday of expiration month.

EXERCISE PRICES
Set at five-point intervals to bracket current index value. New exercise (strike) prices added as index moves.

PREMIUM QUOTATION
Expressed as points (and fractions thereof) where one point equals $100.

MARGIN REQUIREMENTS
Premium plus 10% of the underlying index value (index level times $100) less the amount by which the option is out-of-the-money, or premium plus 2% of underlying index value, whichever is greater.

EXERCISE SETTLEMENT
Cash settlement based on the dollar difference between the index level and the exercise price of the contract multiplied by 100. The index level is determined following the close of trading on the day exercise instructions are submitted.

EXERCISE PROCEDURE American.

TRADING HOURS 10:00 A.M. to 4:10 P.M. EST

Philadelphia Stock Exchange Utility Index

EXCHANGE PHLX

SYMBOL UTY

CONTRACT MULTIPLIER 100

EXPIRATION CYCLE Monthly

EXPIRATION DATE
Saturday following third Friday of expiration month.

EXERCISE PRICES
Set at five-point intervals to bracket current index value. New exercise (strike) prices added as index moves.

PREMIUM QUOTATION
Expressed as points (and fractions thereof) where one point equals $100.

MARGIN REQUIREMENTS
Premium plus 20% of the underlying index value (index level times $100) less the amount by which the option is out-of-the-money, or premium plus 10% of underlying index value, whichever is greater.

EXERCISE SETTLEMENT
Cash settlement based on the dollar difference between the index level and the exercise price of the contract multiplied by 100. The index level is determined following the close of trading on the day exercise instructions are submitted.

EXERCISE PROCEDURE European.

TRADING HOURS 9:30 A.M. to 4:10 P.M. EST

S&P 100 Index

EXCHANGE CBOE

SYMBOL OEX

CONTRACT MULTIPLIER 100

EXPIRATION CYCLE Monthly

EXPIRATION DATE
Saturday following third Friday of expiration month.

EXERCISE PRICES
Set at five-point intervals to bracket current index value. New exercise (strike) prices added as index moves.

PREMIUM QUOTATION
Expressed as points (and fractions thereof) where one point equals $100.

MARGIN REQUIREMENTS
Premium plus 15% of the underlying index value (index level times $100) less the amount by which the option is out-of-the-money, or premium plus 10% of underlying index value, whichever is greater.

EXERCISE SETTLEMENT
Cash settlement based on the dollar difference between the index level and the exercise price of the contract multiplied by 100. The index level is determined following the close of trading on the day exercise instructions are submitted.

EXERCISE PROCEDURE American.

TRADING HOURS 9:30 A.M. to 4:15 P.M. EST

LEAPS - S&P 100 Index

EXCHANGE   CBOE

SYMBOL   OLX ('92 series); OAX ('93 series)

CONTRACT MULTIPLIER   100

EXPIRATION CYCLE   Annually

EXPIRATION DATE
Saturday following third Friday of expiration month.

EXERCISE PRICES
Set at two and one-half point intervals to bracket current index value. New
exercise (strike) prices added as index moves.

PREMIUM QUOTATION
Expressed as points (and fractions thereof) where one point equals $100.

MARGIN REQUIREMENTS
Premium plus 15% of the underlying index value (index level times $100) less
the amount by which the option is out-of-the-money, or premium plus 10% of
underlying index value, whichever is greater.

EXERCISE SETTLEMENT
Cash settlement based on the dollar difference between the index level and the
exercise price of the contract multiplied by 100. The index level is determined
following the close of trading on the day exercise instructions are submitted.

EXERCISE PROCEDURE   American.

TRADING HOURS   9:30 A.M. to 4:15 P.M. EST

S&P 500 Index

EXCHANGE CBOE

SYMBOL SPX

CONTRACT MULTIPLIER 100

EXPIRATION CYCLE Monthly

EXPIRATION DATE
Saturday following third Friday of expiration month.

EXERCISE PRICES
Set at five-point intervals to bracket current index value (twenty-five-point intervals for far month). New exercise (strike) prices added as index moves.

PREMIUM QUOTATION
Expressed as points (and fractions thereof) where one point equals $100.

MARGIN REQUIREMENTS
Premium plus 15% of the underlying index value (index level times $100) less the amount by which the option is out-of-the-money, or premium plus 10% of underlying index value, whichever is greater.

EXERCISE SETTLEMENT
Cash settlement based on the dollar difference between the index level and the exercise price of the contract multiplied by 100. The index level is determined following the close of trading on the day exercise instructions are submitted.

EXERCISE PROCEDURE European.

TRADING HOURS 9:30 A.M. to 4:15 P.M. EST

LEAPS - S&P 500 Index

EXCHANGE CBOE

SYMBOL LSX ('92 series); LSW ('93 series)

CONTRACT MULTIPLIER 100

EXPIRATION CYCLE Annually

EXPIRATION DATE
Saturday following third Friday of expiration month.

EXERCISE PRICES
Set at two and one-half point intervals to bracket current index value. New exercise (strike) prices added as index moves.

PREMIUM QUOTATION
Expressed as points (and fractions thereof) where one point equals $100.

MARGIN REQUIREMENTS
Premium plus 15% of the underlying index value (index level times $100) less the amount by which the option is out-of-the-money, or premium plus 10% of underlying index value, whichever is greater.

EXERCISE SETTLEMENT
Cash settlement based on the dollar difference between the index level and the exercise price of the contract multiplied by 100. The index level is determined following the close of trading on the day exercise instructions are submitted.

EXERCISE PROCEDURE European.

TRADING HOURS 9:30 A.M. to 4:15 P.M. EST

Value Line Composite

EXCHANGE PHLX

SYMBOL VLE

CONTRACT MULTIPLIER 100

EXPIRATION CYCLE Monthly

EXPIRATION DATE
Saturday following third Friday of expiration month.

EXERCISE PRICES
Set at five-point intervals to bracket current index value (twenty-five-point intervals for far month). New exercise (strike) prices added as index moves.

PREMIUM QUOTATION
Expressed as points (and fractions thereof) where one point equals $100.

EXERCISE SETTLEMENT
Cash settlement based on the dollar difference between the index level and the exercise price of the contract multiplied by 100. The index level is determined following the close of trading on the day exercise instructions are submitted.

EXERCISE PROCEDURE European.

TRADING HOURS 9:30 A.M. to 4:15 P.M. EST

Appendix D:
Exchange Addresses

American Stock Exchange
Options Marketing Department
86 Trinity Place
New York, NY 10006
1-800-THE-AMEX
1-800-462-AMEX (within New York)

Chicago Board Options Exchange
LaSalle at Van Buren
Chicago, IL 60605
1-800-OPTIONS

New York Stock Exchange
Options & Index Products
20 Broad Street
New York, NY 10005
1-800-692-6973

Pacific Stock Exchange
Options Marketing
115 Sansome Street 7th Floor
San Francisco, CA 94104
1-800-TALK-PSE

Philadelphia Stock Exchange
1900 Market Street
Philadelphia, PA 19103
1-800-THE-PHLX

Appendix E:
Bibliography

BOOKS

Ansbacher, Max G. *The New Stock Index Market.* New York: Walker & Company, 1983.

Berlin, Howard M. *The Handbook of Financial Market Indexes, Averages and Indicators.* Homewood: Dow Jones Irwin, 1990.

Bishop, Elizabeth, ed. *Indexation.* London: Euromoney Books, 1990.

Blank, Steven C.; Carter, Colin A.; and Schmiesing, Brian H. *Futures & Options Markets.* Englewood Cliffs: Prentice Hall, 1991.

Bookstaber, Richard M. *Option Pricing & Investment Strategies.* Chicago: Probus Publishing Company, 1987.

Brenner, Menachem. *Option Pricing: Theory & Applications.* Lexington: Lexington Books, D.C. Heath & Company, 1983.

Byrne, B. Thomas Jr. *The Stock Index Futures Market.* Chicago: Probus Publishing Company, 1987.

Chance, Don M. *An Introduction to Options and Futures.* New York: The Dryden Press, 1989.

Dodd, Mikel T. *Trading Stock Index Options.* Chicago: Probus Publishing Company, 1988.

Dow Jones & Company Educational Service Bureau. *The Dow Jones Industrial Averages: A Non-Professional's Guide.* New York: Dow Jones & Company, 1983.

Fabozzi, Frank J. and Kipnis, Gregory M., eds. *The Handbook of Stock Index Futures and Options.* Homewood: Dow Jones Irwin, 1989.

Figlewski, Stephen; Silber, William L.; and Subramanyam, Marti G. *Financial Options.* Homewood: Business One Irwin, 1990.

Fried, Sidney. *Investment and Speculation With Warrants, Options, & Convertibles.* Glen Cove: RHM Press, 1989.

Gastineau, Gary L. *The Options Manual.* New York: McGraw Hill, 1988.

Gibson, Rajna. *Option Valuation.* New York: McGraw Hill, 1991.

Hull, John. *Options, Futures, and Other Derivative Securities.* Englewood Cliffs: Prentice Hall, 1989.

Khoury, Sarkis J. *Speculative Markets.* New York: Macmillan Publishing Company, 1984.

Lerner, E.M. *Readings In Financial Analysis And Investment Management.* Homewood: Richard D. Irwin, 1963.

Luskin, Donald L. *Index Options & Futures.* New York: John Wiley & Sons, 1987.

_____. *Portfolio Insurance: A Guide To Dynamic Hedging.* New York: John Wiley & Sons, 1988.

Marshall, John F. *Futures and Options Contracting.* Cincinnati: South Western Publishing Company, 1989.

McMillan, Lawrence G. *Options as a Strategic Investment.* New York: New York Institute of Finance, 1986.

Natenberg, Sheldon. *Option Volatility and Pricing Strategies.* Chicago: Probus Publishing, 1988.

Nix, William E., and Nix, Susan W. *The Dow Jones Irwin Guide to Stock Index Futures and Options.* Homewood: Dow Jones Irwin, 1984.

Options Clearing Corporation. *Characteristics and Risks of Standardized Options.* Chicago: Options Clearing Corporation, 1987.

_____. *Directory of Exchange Listed Options.* Chicago: Options Clearing Corporation, 1990.

Options Institute. *Options: Essential Concepts and Trading Strategies.* Homewood: Business One Irwin, 1990.

Petzel, Todd E. *Financial Futures and Options.* New York: Quorum Books, 1989.

Pierce, Phyllis S., ed. *The Dow Jones Averages 1885-1980.* Homewood: Dow Jones Irwin, 1982.

Ritchken, Peter. *Options: Theory, Strategy and Applications.* Glenview: Scott, Foresman and Company, 1987.

Rubinstein, Mark, and Cox, John C. *Options Markets.* Englewood Cliffs: Prentice-Hall, 1985.

Smith, Courtney. *Option Strategies: Profit Making Techniques for Stock, Stock/Index and Commodity Options.* New York: John Wiley & Sons, 1987.

Spicer & Oppenheim CPA. *Taxes and Investing: An Updated Guide for the Individual Investor.* New York: New York Stock Exchange, 1988.

Standard & Poor's Corporation. *S&P 500 1990 Directory.* New York: Standard & Poor's Corporation, 1990.

Stillman, Richard J. *Dow Jones Industrial Average: History and Role in an Investment Strategy.* Homewood: Dow Jones Irwin, 1986.

Strong, Robert A. *Speculative Markets: Options, Futures and Hard Assets.* Chicago: Longman Financial Services Publishing, 1989.

ARTICLES

Abbott, Walter F. "A Look At The Dow From An Historical View." *AAII Journal* (September, 1987).

Balch, W. F. "Market Guides: Indexes Of Stock Prices Lately Have Multiplied." *Barron's* (September 26, 1966).

Bonham, Howard B. Jr. "Equity Investment Return in 1970: A Statistical Projection of the Dow Jones Industrial Average." *Financial Analysts Journal* (May-June, 1968).

Butler, H.L. Jr., and Allen, J. D. "The Dow Jones Industrial Average Re-Reexamined." *Financial Analysts Journal* (November-December, 1979).

Butler, H.L. Jr., and Decker, M.B. "A Security Check on the Dow Jones Industrial Average." *Financial Analysts Journal* (February, 1953).

Butler, H.L. Jr., and DeMong, R.F. "The Changing Dow Jones Industrial Average." *Financial Analysts Journal* (July-August, 1986).

Carter, E.E., and Cohen, K.J. "Stock Averages, Stock Splits and Bias." *Financial Analysts Journal* (May-June, 1967).

_____. "Bias In The DJIA Caused By Stock Splits." *Financial Analysts Journal* (December, 1966).

Cootner, Paul H. "Stock Market Indexes: Fallacies and Illusions." *Commercial and Financial Chronicle* (September 27, 1966).

Fisher, Lawrence. "Some New Stock Market Indexes." *Journal of Business Security Prices: A Supplement* (January, 1966).

Gordon, C.E. II, and Leuthold, S.C. "Margin For Error: The American Stock Exchange Index Has Exceeded It." *Barron's* (March 1, 1971).

Kekish, Bohdan J. "Moody's Averages." *Financial Analysts Journal* (May-June, 1967).

Latane, H.A.; Tuttle, D.L.; and Young, W.E. "Market Indexes And Their Implications For Portfolio Management." *Financial Analysts Journal* (September-October, 1971).

Legan, Robert W. "The DJIA At 2100 In Ten Years." *Financial Analysts Journal* (January-February, 1969).

Leuthold, S.C., and Blaich, K.I. "Warped Yardstick." *Barron's* (September, 18, 1972).

Milne, Robert D. "The Dow Jones Industrial Average Re-Examined." *Financial Analysts Journal* (November-December, 1966).

Molodovsky, Nicholas. "Building A Stock Market Measure—A Case Study." *Financial Analysts Journal* (May-June, 1967).

Neubert, Albert S. "The S&P 500." *AAII Journal* (January 1987).

Reilly, Frank K. "Price Changes in NYSE, AMEX, and OTC Stocks Compared." *Financial Analysts Journal* (March-April, 1971).

Rubinstein, Mark. "Alternative Paths to Portfolio Insurance." *Financial Analysts Journal* (July-August, 1985).

Rubinstein, Mark, and Leland, Hane E. "Replicating Options With Positions In Stock and Cash." *Financial Analysts Journal* (July-August, 1981).

Rudd, Andrew T. "The Revised Dow Jones Industrial Average: New Wine in Old Bottles?" *Financial Analysts Journal* (November-December, 1979).

Schellbach, Lewis L. "Yardsticks For The Market." *The Analysts Journal* (November, 1955).

_____. "When Did The DJIA Top 1200?" *Financial Analysts Journal* (May-June, 1967).

Schloss, Walter J. "The Dow Jones Industrial Average Amended." *The Analysts Journal* (February, 1953).

Schoomer, B. Alva Jr. "The American Stock Exchange Index System." *Financial Analysts Journal* (May-June, 1967).

Shaw, R.B. "The Dow Jones Industrials vs. The Dow Jones Industrial Average." *Financial Analysts Journal* (November, 1955).

West, S., and Miller, N. "Why The New NYSE Common Stock Indexes?" *Financial Analysts Journal* (May-June, 1967).

White, James A. "Will The Real S&P 500 Please Stand Up?" *Wall Street Journal* (January 26, 1989).

UNPUBLISHED WORKS

Brenner, Menachem; Courtadon, George; and Subramanyam, Marti G. "The Valuation of Stock Index Options." Working paper, 1987.
Kolb, Robert W. "Options: An Introduction." Book manuscript, 1990.

Appendix F:
Glossary

Aggregate exercise price: The total dollars required to exercise an option contract. It is the exercise price multiplied by the number of units of the underlying asset covered by the contract.

American option: A put or call option that can be exercised at any time prior to expiration. This is in contrast to a European option that can be exercised only on the expiration date. The distinction is important to theoreticians since the latter are usually easier to analyze.

Arbitrage: The simultaneous purchase and sale of identical, substantially identical, or equivalent assets in one or more than one market with the intent of capturing the price differential as a riskless profit.

Asked: The price at which an asset can be acquired from a potential seller. The asked price is usually quoted with the bid price, the price at which an asset can be sold to a potential buyer. The difference between the bid price and the asked price is known as the bid-asked spread.

Assignment: Notification to a writer by the Options Clearing Corporation that the terms of an option contract must be fulfilled. For a call writer this is an obligation to sell stock at the exercise price. For a put seller this is an obligation to buy stock at the exercise price.

At-the-money: The price relationship where the exercise price of the option is equal to the market price of the underlying security.

Automatic exercise: Exchange implemented exercise at expiration of in-the-money options in the absence of specific instructions by the option holder.

Beta: A numerical measure of the sensitivity of movements in the price of a stock to movements in the overall market as reflected by a broad-based index such as the S&P 500 or the NYSE Composite Index. A beta of 1.10 indicates that the stock will rise or fall 10% more than a corresponding move in the market.

Bid: The price at which an asset can be sold to a potential buyer. The bid price is usually quoted with the asked price, the price at which an asset can be purchased from a potential seller. The difference between the bid price and the asked price is known as the bid-asked spread.

Black-Scholes formula: A mathematical model derived from option theory used to calculated the price at which an option *should* trade. The model is one means of determining option fair value.

Breakeven point: The stock price (or prices) at which an investment strategy produces zero net gain or loss.

Bullish: A market outlook anticipating rising prices.

Buy in: An involuntary repurchase of shares previously sold short because of the inability of the brokerage firm to retain the position.

Bearish: A market outlook anticipating declining prices.

Call option: A contract granting the privilege but not the obligation to purchase an asset at a specified price for a specified period of time after which the contract is worthless.

Cash settlement: Fulfillment of the terms of exercise for an option contract not by delivery of underlying security but rather by appropriate debits and credits of the amount by which the option is in-the-money.

Class: As a group, all the put option contracts on the same underlying security or all the call option contracts on the same underlying security.

Closing price: The last price at which transactions are made prior to the closing bell.

Closing purchase transaction: Termination of a long option position by an offsetting sale.

Closing transaction: The termination of an open position by its corresponding offset. For option buyers this transaction is a closing sale. For option sellers this transaction is a closing purchase.

Collateral: Cash or securities (including T-bills) deposited with a broker to guarantee performance on short positions (stocks and options).

Contingent claim: A term used interchangeably for an option or any security having the features of an option such as a warrant, convertible bond, callable bond, or convertible preferred stock. Fulfillment of these contracts requires performance by both parties involved. The option writer has the liability to deliver stock in the case of calls or to receive stock in the case of puts. Those obligations are contingent upon conditions that the buyer must meet; namely, paying the exercise price in the case of calls or delivering stock in the case of puts.

Contract size: The specification of the amount of the asset optioned by a put or call contract. For equity options this is usually 100 shares of the underlying stock unless adjusted because of a stock dividend or a stock split. For index options, the size or underlying value is determined by the index multiplier and the level of the underlying index.

Conversion: A combination position consisting of three elements: long stock and long puts (that is, long a synthetic call) plus the sale of a call. Conversions are virtually riskless arbitrages permitting traders to capitalize on price discrepancies between securities supplemented by the dividend received from the stock.

Convertible security: Bonds or preferred stock with special provision that they can be exchanged for other securities—usually a common stock issue—at the holder's option.

Cover: To buy back as a closing transaction an option that was previously sold.

Covered writing: An investment strategy in which common stock is purchased and call options are sold on a one-for-one basis.

Credit: A positive account balance resulting from any transaction bringing money into an account such as a deposit or an option opening sale transaction.

Deep-in-the-money: An alternative description for options having substantial intrinsic value. For calls it is the price relationship where the stock price is far above the exercise price. For puts it is the condition where the stock price is well below the exercise price.

Delivery: The transfer of securities when an option is exercised. A call writer who is assigned delivers stock to the call buyer who exercised. A put buyer who exercises delivers stock to the put writer who is assigned.

Delta: The option price change resulting from a one point change in the price of the underlying stock. Also called the hedge ratio.

Discount option: An option selling below its intrinsic value. The premium plus the exercise price is less than the price of the underlying security.

Downside breakeven: The price below which an investment strategy generates losses.

Downside protection: The cushion against falling prices provided by the premium received from the sale of call options.

Downstairs: Trading by members on the exchange floor. As opposed to upstairs which is trading directed from a remote location. Both participants have advantages and disadvantages. Which party has the edge is the subject of continuous debate.

Early exercise: The exercise of an option contract prior to its expiration date.

Escrow receipt: A bank-issued voucher verifying ownership of securities thus permitting the sale of calls in a brokerage account without the need to post additional collateral.

European option: A put or call that can be exercised only on the expiration date. In contrast to an American option that can be exercised at any time prior to expiration.

Exercise: Assignment of an option contract; that is, sale of stock to the writer in the case of puts or purchase of stock from the writer in the case of calls.

Exercise limit: The total number of puts or calls on the same underlying instrument that a single investor or group of investors acting in concert may exercise during any five consecutive business days.

Exercise price: The price at which the underlying instrument changes hands when an option contract is exercised. Also called the strike price.

Expiration date: The day on which the option contract terminates and thereafter becomes null and void. For listed options the expiration date is the Saturday following the third Friday of the month.

Extrinsic value: The value of an option over and above the intrinsic value. Extrinsic value is also called time value. The price of an out-of-the-money option is entirely extrinsic value.

Fair value: The price at which an option should trade in an efficient market as predicted by option theory.

Floor broker: An exchange member who trades on the exchange floor executing orders for non-members.

Floor trader: An exchanged member who buys and sells for his own account fulfilling the function of a market maker.

Front running: A transaction in options based on advance knowledge of a forthcoming transaction in stocks that will affect the options price favorably.

Fungibility: Complete interchangeability resulting from the standardization of option contracts and the severance of the direct link between a buyer and a seller as made possible by the Options Clearing Corporation. An opening transaction can be offset by a closing transaction in an identical contract.

Futures contract: An exchanged traded commitment with standardized terms (including quality, quantity, time, and location) to make or accept delivery of a commodity at a price agreed upon at the time the contract was traded.

Hedge: A position in two related securities, such that the risk in one position partially or totally offsets the risk in the other.

Hedge ratio: The fractional price change in an option resulting from a one point change in the price of the underlying stock. Also called delta.

Historical volatility: Volatility measured from a sequence of past security prices.

Holder: The owner of a security.

Implied volatility: That value of volatility that, when inserted into an option model, produces a solution that is the current traded price of the option. It is the volatility that the market currently assigns to the underlying instrument as implied by the market price of the option.

Institution: A large organization that commands vast resources and trades in large volumes such as a pension fund, mutual fund, bank, or insurance company.

Initial margin requirement: The minimum margin that must be posted when entering an investment position.

In-the-money: An option having intrinsic value. Call options are in-the-money when the price of the underlying instrument is above the option exercise price. Put options are in-the-money when the price of the underlying instrument is below the option exercise price.

Intrinsic value: The cash value of the option. It is the amount that, when combined with the exercise price, can be applied in acquiring the underlying asset. For calls, the intrinsic value is the stock price minus the exercise price. For puts, the intrinsic value is the exercise price minus the stock price. In other words, it is the amount by which an option is in-the-money.

Leg in: Non-simultaneous execution of transactions in a multiple position strategy. The objective is to establish one portion and to complete others at more favorable prices.

Leverage: The magnification of the potential (both risk and reward) of an investment when a given amount of money controls assets of substantially greater value.

Limit order: An order to buy of sell at a specified price or better.

Liquid market: A market characterized by high volume of trading, narrow bid-asked spreads, and depth (meaningful size at both bid and asked prices). Buying and selling in quantity can be accomplished with perturbing prices.

Listed option: A put or call with standardized terms traded on a national securities exchange.

Long: A position of ownership resulting from acquisition of an asset. An investor who is long will make money if the asset rises in price. As opposed to short.

Margin: The equity which must be posted by an investor to collateralize an investment position.

Market maker: An exchange member responsible for maintaining liquidity by making bids and offers for his own account in the absence of public orders. Several market makers are usually assigned to particular security.

Market-maker-system: An approach to implementing trading on the exchange floor where liquidity is provided by many competing market makers. As opposed to specialist system.

Model: A mathematical formula derived from the theory of options and finance, the solution of which gives the price at which an option should trade.

Naked option: An option position either long or short that is unhedged.

Net margin requirement: The collateral required to finance an option sale after deducting the premium received.

Neutral: A market outlook anticipating relatively unchanged prices.

Neutral hedge: A hedge balanced to give highest return when the underlying security price remains unchanged. The upside and downside breakeven points are generally equidistant from the entry price.

Offsetting transaction: A transaction that terminates an option position either long or short. An opening sale transaction is offset by a closing purchase. An opening purchase is offset by a closing sale.

Open interest: The number of option contracts outstanding; that is, those not eliminated by exercise, assignment, or closing transactions.

Opening purchase transaction: A trade establishing a long position in an option, either a put or a call.

Opening sale transaction: A trade establishing a short position in an option, either a put or a call.

Opening transaction: A transaction establishing a new option position. An opening purchase adds a long position. An opening sale adds a short option position.

Option: A contract granting the privilege but not the obligation to buy or sell at a particular price for a specified period of time.

Option period: The lifetime of the option as specified in the contract and within which the buyer must exercise or lose the privilege.

Option price curve: A graph of the expected track or trajectory along which an option price will move in response to a changed in the price of the underlying security. Because option price is a function of time, the curve is valid only for a short period after which it must be recomputed.

Options Clearing Corporation: An organization owned by the various exchanges that trades listed option contracts. It is an intermediary, acting as issuer of all option contracts and also as the guarantor of each of the contracts.

Options exchange: One of the securities exchanges authorized to trade listed options.

Out-of-the-money: An option for which the intrinsic value is zero. Call options are out-of-the-money when the price of the underlying security is below the options exercise price. Put options are out-of-the-money when the price of the underlying security is above the option exercise price.

Overvalued: Priced in excess of the expected price as predicted by experience or an option valuation model.

Parity: The market price for an in-the-money option that is equal to its intrinsic value. The time value of the option is zero.

Position limit: The maximum number of options on the same side of the market (calls held plus puts written, or puts held plus calls written) for a single underlying instrument that may be held or written by a single investor or group of investors acting in concert.

Premium: The price of an option. Infrequently the term is used interchangeably with time value.

Profit profile: A graph of table showing projected returns for an investment strategy over a range of prices in the underlying security.

Put: An option granting the holder the privilege but not the obligation to sell the underlying security at a particular price for a specified period of time.

Ratio writing: An investment strategy involving sale of options in excess of those covered by a long position.

Return: The total change in value of an investment including appreciation and yield (dividend or interest).

Reverse conversion: A combination position consisting of three elements—short stock and long calls (that is, long a synthetic put) plus the sale of a put. Reverse conversions are virtually riskless arbitrages permitting traders to capitalize on price discrepancies between securities while earning interest on the credit balance resulting from the short sale. An important adjunct to reverse conversions is the creation of puts that might otherwise be illiquid and therefore unavailable.

Rolling: Repositioning by switching from one option into another having a different exercise price or expiration date. See also rolling up, rolling down and rolling forward.

193

Rolling down: The simultaneous closing of an option position at one strike price and opening of a substantially identical position at a lower strike price.

Rolling forward: The simultaneous closing of an option position in one expiration month and opening of a substantially identical position in an expiration month further out.

Rolling up: The simultaneous closing of an option position at one strike price and opening of a substantially identical position at a higher strike price.

Securities & Exchange Commission (SEC): An agency of the federal government that regulates and oversees the securities markets in the United States.

Series: All option contracts of the same class on the same underlying security having the same exercise price, expiration date, and unit of trading.

Short option position: The position of the writer or seller of a put or call.

Short sale: The sale of a borrowed security in anticipation of falling prices. If the drop materializes the securities are repurchased (covered) at the lower level and the profit is the difference between the original sale price and the subsequent purchase price.

Specialist: An exchange member responsible for making markets in specific securities and for keeping the book of public orders. This entails maintaining a liquid and continuous market buying and selling for his own account in the absence of public orders.

Speculator: An investor willing to assume excessive risk in search of disproportionate capital gain.

Spread: An option hedge consisting of a long position in one or more options and an offsetting short position in options on the same security but of a different series, a different strike price, or a different expiration date.

Standard deviation: A statistical calculation that measures the tendency of the data in a distribution to cluster about a mean value.

Stock index futures: A standard futures contract requiring purchase or delivery of the cash value of a stock index at some specified point in the future.

Straddle: An option hedge position consisting of a put and a call on the same underlying instrument at the same exercise price and with the same expiration date. A straddle is purchased if both positions are long. The objective is to profit from a major move in the market in either direction. A straddle is sold if both option positions are short. The objective is to profit from a stagnant market.

Straddle buying: The purchase of a put and a call on the same underlying instrument with the same strike price and the same expiration date executed in anticipation of major price move (in either direction).

Straddle selling: The sale of a put and a call on the same underlying instrument with the same strike price and the same expiration date executed in anticipation of a stagnant market.

Strike price: The price at which the underlying asset will change hands when an option is exercised. Also called the exercise price.

Strike price interval: The distance between striking prices in an option series. For equity options the interval is 5 points for stocks selling up to $100 and 10 points for stocks selling up to $200. For traditional index options the interval is always 5 points. For long term index options the interval varies.

Synthetic call: A combination position consisting of long stock in conjunction with puts purchased on the same stock. The profit profile is equivalent for outright purchase of a call option.

Synthetic put: A combination position consisting of short stock in conjunction with calls purchased on the same stock. The profit profile is equivalent for outright purchase of a put option.

Systematic risk: That part of total risk attributable to the overall influence of the market.

Terms: The provisions of an option contract including the underlying instrument, the exercise price, the expiration date, and the method of settlement.

Theoretical value: The price of an option as computed by an option valuation model.

Time value: That component of option premium that exceeds intrinsic value. It is the amount by which the market price of an option exceeds the amount that could be realized if the option were exercised.

Trading pit: A specific location on the exchange floor designated for trading in a particular option.

Transaction costs: Charges associated with executing a trade including commissions and exchange fees. It also includes a penalty imposed by the existence of the bid-asked spread.

Type: The classification of an option as a put or a call.

Uncovered: Options in an unhedged context. Equivalent to naked options.

Underlying security: The asset which can be purchased or sold in accordance with terms of the option contract.

Undervalued: Selling at a price below that predicted by an option valuation model.

Unsystematic risk: That part of total risk attributable to a particular firm and its industry group.

Upstairs: Trading directed from locations other than the exchange floor. As opposed to downstairs trading which is trading on the exchange floor.

Volatility: A measure of a stock's propensity to change in price over a period of time, generally computed from historical data. More precisely, it is a statistical calculation; namely, the annualized standard deviation of security price changes.

Warrant: An option to buy stock (generally that of the issuer) at a specified price for a particular period of time. Warrants are similar to call options.

Wasting asset: An investment having a finite life where payoff depends upon time for a workout. Thus, value is proportional to time.

Whipsaw: A rapid sequence of price reversals always out of synchronization with the investor's position.

Writer: The seller or grantor of an option contract.

Appendix G: Cumulative Normal Distribution

The cumulative normal density function N(d) is a statistical concept. It is the area under the normal curve below d. In the Black-Scholes model, the underlying security's return is asumed to be lognormally distributed; therefore, N(d) is the probability that, in a normal distribution, a deviation less than d will occur. Tables for the cumulative normal distribution model are included in most statistical texts. An abbreviated table is provided in Exhibit G-3.

From the sample solution for the Black-Scholes model given in Exhibit 7-5 $d_1 = 0.1871$ and $d_2 = 0.1364$. Using the table in Exhibit G-3, $N(d_1) = 0.5742$ and $N(d_2) = 0.5543$.

The function N(d) can also be calculated using the mathematical approximation provided in Exhibit G-1. Programmed into a computer or pocket calculator, this formula permits a rapid solution of the Black-Scholes model. Using the approximation, Exhibit G-2 shows calculations for the values of the $N(d_1)$ and $N(d_2)$ required for the sample solution of the Black-Scholes model presented in Exhibit 7-5.

EXHIBIT G-1

Mathematical Approximation for N(d)

$$N(d) = \left[1 - \left(\frac{1}{\sqrt{2\pi}} e^{-d2/2} \right) (.4361836k - .1201676k^2 + .9372980k^3) \right]$$

$$= \left[1 - (.3989)(e^{-d2/2})(.4361836k - .1201676k^2 + .9372980k^3) \right]$$

$$k = \frac{1}{1 + .33267d}$$

Source: Abramowitz, Milton and Stegun, Irene A., eds. Handbook of Mathematical Functions, National Bureau of Standards, Applied Mathematics Series 55, Superintendent of Documents, Washington, D.C., 1972.

EXHIBIT G-2

Solving for N(d) Using Mathematical Approximation

d_1	=	0.1871	d_2	=	0.1364
k_1	=	$\dfrac{1}{1 + (0.33267)(0.1871)}$	k_2	=	0.9566
	=	0.9414	k_2^2	=	0.9151
k_1^2	=	0.8862	k_2^3	=	0.8754
k_1^3	=	0.8343	$N(d_2)$	=	0.5580
$e^{-d2/2}$	=	0.9826			
$\dfrac{1}{\sqrt{2\pi}}$	=	0.3989			
$N(d_1)$	=	0.5742			

EXHIBIT G-3

Cumulative Normal Probability Distribution Where d1 or d2 is Positive

d	.00	.01	.02	.03	.04	.05	.06	.07	.08	.09
0.00	.5000	.5040	.5080	.5120	.5159	.5199	.5239	.5279	.5319	.5358
0.10	.5398	.5438	.5478	.5517	.5557	.5596	.5636	.5675	.5714	.5753
0.20	.5793	.5832	.5871	.5909	.5948	.5987	.6026	.6064	.6103	.6141
0.30	.6179	.6217	.6255	.6293	.6331	.6368	.6406	.6443	.6480	.6517
0.40	.6554	.6591	.6628	.6664	.6700	.6736	.6772	.6808	.6844	.6879
0.50	.6915	.6950	.6985	.7019	.7054	.7088	.7123	.7157	.7190	.7224
0.60	.7257	.7291	.7324	.7356	.7389	.7421	.7454	.7486	.7517	.7549
0.70	.7580	.7611	.7642	.7673	.7703	.7734	.7764	.7793	.7823	.7852
0.80	.7881	.7910	.7939	.7967	.7995	.8023	.8051	.8078	.8106	.8133
0.90	.8159	.8186	.8212	.8238	.8264	.8289	.8315	.8340	.8365	.8389
1.00	.8413	.8437	.8461	.8485	.8508	.8531	.8554	.8577	.8599	.8621
1.10	.8643	.8665	.8686	.8708	.8729	.8749	.8770	.8790	.8810	.8830
1.20	.8849	.8869	.8888	.8906	.8925	.8943	.8962	.8980	.8997	.9015
1.30	.9032	.9049	.9066	.9082	.9099	.9115	.9131	.9147	.9162	.9177
1.40	.9192	.9207	.9222	.9236	.9251	.9265	.9279	.9292	.9306	.9319
1.50	.9332	.9345	.9357	.9370	.9382	.9394	.9406	.9418	.9429	.9441
1.60	.9452	.9463	.9474	.9484	.9495	.9505	.9515	.9525	.9535	.9545
1.70	.9554	.9564	.9573	.9582	.9591	.9599	.9608	.9616	.9625	.9633
1.80	.9641	.9649	.9656	.9664	.9671	.9678	.9686	.9693	.9699	.9706
1.90	.9713	.9719	.9726	.9732	.9738	.9744	.9750	.9756	.9761	.9767
2.00	.9772	.9778	.9783	.9788	.9793	.9798	.9803	.9808	.9812	.9817
2.10	.9821	.9826	.9830	.9834	.9838	.9842	.9846	.9850	.9854	.9857
2.20	.9861	.9864	.9868	.9871	.9875	.9878	.9881	.9884	.9887	.9890
2.30	.9893	.9896	.9898	.9901	.9904	.9906	.9909	.9911	.9913	.9916
2.40	.9918	.9920	.9922	.9925	.9927	.9929	.9931	.9932	.9934	.9936
2.50	.9938	.9940	.9941	.9943	.9945	.9946	.9948	.9949	.9951	.9952
2.60	.9953	.9955	.9956	.9957	.9959	.9960	.9961	.9962	.9963	.9964
2.70	.9965	.9966	.9967	.9968	.9969	.9970	.9971	.9972	.9973	.9974
2.80	.9974	.9975	.9976	.9977	.9977	.9978	.9979	.9979	.9980	.9981
2.90	.9981	.9982	.9982	.9983	.9984	.9984	.9985	.9985	.9986	.9986
3.00	.9986	.9987	.9987	.9988	.9988	.9989	.9989	.9989	.9990	.9990

EXHIBIT G-3 (Continued)

Cumulative Normal Probability Distribution Where d1 or d2 is Positive

d	.00	.01	.02	.03	.04	.05	.06	.07	.08	.09
—3.00	.0014	.0013	.0013	.0012	.0012	.0011	.0011	.0011	.0010	.0010
—2.90	.0019	.0010	.0018	.0017	.0016	.0016	.0015	.0015	.0014	.0014
—2.80	.0026	.0025	.0024	.0023	.0023	.0022	.0021	.0021	.0020	.0019
—2.70	.0035	.0034	.0033	.0032	.0031	.0030	.0029	.0028	.0027	.0026
—2.60	.0047	.0045	.0044	.0043	.0041	.0040	.0039	.0038	.0037	.0036
—2.50	.0062	.0060	.0059	.0057	.0055	.0054	.0052	.0051	.0049	.0048
—2.40	.0082	.0080	.0078	.0075	.0073	.0071	.0069	.0068	.0066	.0064
—2.30	.0107	.0104	.0102	.0099	.0096	.0094	.0091	.0089	.0087	.0084
—2.20	.0139	.0136	.0132	.0129	.0125	.0122	.0119	.0116	.0113	.0110
—2.10	.0179	.0174	.0170	.0166	.0162	.0158	.0154	.0150	.0146	.0143
—2.00	.0228	.0222	.0217	.0212	.0207	.0202	.0197	.0192	.0188	.0183
—1.90	.0287	.0281	.0274	.0268	.0262	.0256	.0250	.0244	.0239	.0233
—1.80	.0359	.0351	.0344	.0336	.0329	.0322	.0314	.0307	.0301	.0294
—1.70	.0446	.0436	.0427	.0418	.0409	.0401	.0392	.0384	.0375	.0367
—1.60	.0548	.0537	.0526	.0516	.0505	.0495	.0485	.0475	.0465	.0455
—1.50	.0668	.0655	.0643	.0630	.0618	.0606	.0594	.0582	.0571	.0559
—1.40	.0808	.0793	.0778	.0764	.0749	.0735	.0721	.0708	.0694	.0681
—1.30	.0968	.0951	.0934	.0918	.0901	.0885	.0869	.0853	.0838	.0823
—1.20	.1151	.1131	.1112	.1094	.1075	.1057	.1038	.1020	.1003	.0985
—1.10	.1357	.1335	.1314	.1292	.1271	.1251	.1230	.1210	.1190	.1170
—1.00	.1587	.1563	.1539	.1515	.1492	.1469	.1446	.1423	.1401	.1379
—.90	.1841	.1814	.1788	.1762	.1736	.1711	.1685	.1660	.1635	.1611
—.80	.2119	.2090	.2061	.2033	.2005	.1977	.1949	.1922	.1894	.1867
—.70	.2420	.2389	.2358	.2327	.2297	.2266	.2236	.2207	.2177	.2148
—.60	.2743	.2709	.2676	.2644	.2611	.2579	.2546	.2514	.2483	.2451
—.50	.3085	.3050	.3015	.2981	.2946	.2912	.2877	.2843	.2810	.2776
—.40	.3446	.3409	.3372	.3336	.3300	.3264	.3228	.3192	.3156	.3121
—.30	.3821	.3783	.3745	.3707	.3669	.3632	.3594	.3557	.3520	.3483
—.20	.4207	.4168	.4129	.4091	.4052	.4013	.3974	.3936	.3897	.3859
—.10	.4602	.4562	.4522	.4483	.4443	.4404	.4364	.4325	.4286	.4247
0.00	.5000	.4960	.4920	.4880	.4841	.4801	.4761	.4721	.4681	.4642

Source: Labuszewski, John and Sinquefield, Jeanne Cairns. Inside the Commodity Option Markets. New York: John Wiley & Sons, Inc., 1985.

Index